# ENVOY
## OF THE
# MESSIAH

# ENVOY OF THE MESSIAH

## On Acts of the Apostles 16–28

### Stephen Pimentel

**With a Foreword by Steve Ray**

EMMAUS
ROAD
PUBLISHING

Steubenville, Ohio
A Division of Catholics
United for the Faith

Emmaus Road Publishing
827 North Fourth Street
Steubenville, Ohio 43952

Library of Congress Control Number: 2005929579
ISBN 1-931018-30-8

Cover design and layout by
Beth Hart

On the Cover
*The sermon of Saint Paul at Ephesus* (Acts of the Apostles)
Eustache Lesueur
© Erich Lessing / Art Resource, NY

*Dedicated to*

*Zelie Elizabeth,*
*Josephine Grace,*
*Rosa Mariana, and*
*Elizabeth Grace*


*May the grace of your baptism*
*take root in your hearts*
*and ever flourish*
*that you may be counted*
*among the saints.*

*And now I stand here on trial*
*for hope in the promise made by God to our fathers,*
*to which our twelve tribes hope to attain,*
*as they earnestly worship night and day.*
*—Acts 26:6–7*

# The Travel Areas of the Acts of the Apostles

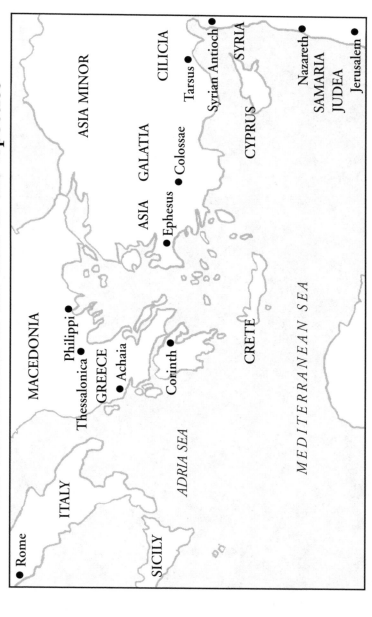

# TABLE OF CONTENTS

# FOREWORD

The inspired account of the beginnings of the Church is commonly called the Acts of the Apostles. But the title seems misleading, and the story has no end. It does not recount the acts of *all* the apostles, and what it *does* tell us is only fragmentary and partial. Early on Peter disappears from its pages and Paul's final years are never discussed. And what of Andrew, John, Matthew, Thomas, Philip, Matthias, and the rest of the apostles?

The story of the early Church is really the story of the Holy Spirit and how He hovered over the first three decades following the death, Resurrection, and Ascension of our Lord Jesus Christ. Though the Holy Spirit is the soul of the Church and ever-present, we only see brief glimpses as He flutters over select high points of those foundational years. The Acts of the Apostles, as we know the story today, is the Holy Spirit's account of what is important for the Church to know about her miraculous beginnings, and it was Saint Luke who penned these inspired and immortal words.

Two men—a fisherman and a scholar—fill most of its pages. One smelled of fish and the other of books, but both were consumed with the Spirit of God and became founders of the Church. Both spilled their blood as martyrs for the new Faith, and both took the Good News of Jesus Christ outside the boundaries of Israel and opened the door of salvation to the world.

Paul must have worn out many sandals during his travels. It is estimated that he traveled over six thousand miles, and most of these journeys are discussed and studied here by Stephen Pimentel, a capable author. In his earlier work, *Witnesses of the Messiah,* Stephen took us on a journey through the first half of the Acts of the Apostles and now he takes us on an intelligent, fast moving, and insightful adventure through the second half of the story.

Acts 1–15 covers the early years of Peter in the Church and has affectionately been called "The Acts of Peter." Acts 16–28 covers the high points of Paul's early ministry and has been referred to as "The Acts of Paul." Though each section only hits the high points of an intense and crucial period of history, they do pull back the curtain to reveal a glimpse of the inner workings of the Holy Spirit and the birth of the Church.

Paul was a man of remarkable strength, insights, and perseverance. He was single-minded and gave his life to serving and suffering for his Messiah like few in history have every matched. He is a theologian *par excellence* and arguably the greatest missionary of all time. He had a drive and a passion for the truth that few could keep up with. It is why we can admire Luke, Timothy, and a few others who stayed with him to the end—at least for the history we have recorded in the New Testament.

Having walked in the footprints of Paul along the roads and in most of the cities he traveled, I am thoroughly impressed with this champion of the faith. I also have come down the wall of Damascus in a basket and fallen off a horse in the desert; floated on driftwood in the Mediterranean; and meditated at the location where Paul's head was eventually severed from his body.

The walls of Damascus are about three stories high. I nervously dangled in a basket in the daylight; Paul came down at night. I realized how tough and heroic he really was. In each of these locations I read the applicable passages from the Bible and meditated on the life and teaching of this wiry and brilliant man.

Paul was in constant danger. Very few wanted to hear this tenacious Jew preach. Most thought he was simply promoting a Jewish heresy. Without fear or hesitation Paul would stand before Jews or Gentiles and proclaim the Gospel of Jesus Christ—the Lord and the Jewish Messiah. Often the result of this bold proclamation was confrontation and bodily harm. Once Paul was stoned, and those who hurled the rocks left him outside the city gates covered with blood and a pile of rocks. They left him for dead. But whether he barely survived or whether he was raised from the dead, Paul got up and went back into the city. Talk about tough and fearless!

There was one particular time I really related to the life and dangers of Saint Paul. While filming I used the name "Jesus" at the Western Wall. I was addressing the video camera and commented on how Paul and Jesus both loved the temple. Two Hassidic Jews heard me say "Jesus" and, because of the Name, they immediately began to tremble and interfere in our filming. One stood in front of the camera and the other confronted me face-to-face. They argued with me and my crew. They said I could not use "the name of that man" here. I said I had permission to film our documentary, and it was necessary to use the name of Jesus. They called the police, a rabbi, and then a crowd quickly gathered. The air was thick enough to cut it with a knife. Anger filled the crowd, and I realized that had it been an earlier time—like the time of Saint Paul—I could have easily been arrested, whipped, beaten, or even stoned. Paul suffered these humiliations over and over again until his final martyrdom in Rome, along with Peter, around AD 67.

Earlier I said the Book of Acts had an unsatisfactory ending—actually no ending. It tells us nothing of the other apostles. Peter disappears from the scene, and Luke tells us nothing of Paul's last years. His life and ministry continued on for many years after Acts and before the sword finally fell in AD 67. Why did Luke leave us with an uncompleted story? I realized early on that the story could not have an end because the Holy Spirit did not discontinue His work at the end of Acts 28. He continues working to this very day. The Acts of the Apostles—really, the "Acts of the Holy Spirit"—does not end until Jesus comes again.

Stephen Pimentel's book takes you though the recorded travels and teachings of Saint Paul as revealed by Luke. He provides interesting insights and theological understanding useful to both the average reader and the scholar. This book is easy to read, yet full of helpful information and Scriptural detail. In fact, it's too bad we can't insert most of this book into our Bibles as footnotes.

Steve Ray
www.CatholicConvert.com

# ABBREVIATIONS

**Old Testament**
Gen./Genesis
Ex./Exodus
Lev./Leviticus
Num./Numbers
Deut./Deuteronomy
Josh./Joshua
Judg./Judges
Ruth/Ruth
1 Sam./1 Samuel
2 Sam./2 Samuel
1 Kings/1 Kings
2 Kings/2 Kings
1 Chron./1 Chronicles
2 Chron./2 Chronicles
Ezra/Ezra
Neh./Nehemiah
Tob./Tobit
Jud./Judith
Esther/Esther
Job/Job
Ps./Psalms
Prov./Proverbs
Eccles./Ecclesiastes
Song/Song of Solomon
Wis./Wisdom
Sir./Sirach (Ecclesiasticus)
Is./Isaiah
Jer./Jeremiah
Lam./Lamentations
Bar./Baruch
Ezek./Ezekiel
Dan./Daniel
Hos./Hosea

Joel/Joel
Amos/Amos
Obad./Obadiah
Jon./Jonah
Mic./Micah
Nahum/Nahum
Hab./Habakkuk
Zeph./Zephaniah
Hag./Haggai
Zech./Zechariah
Mal./Malachi
1 Mac./1 Maccabees
2 Mac./2 Maccabees

**New Testament**
Mt./Matthew
Mk./Mark
Lk./Luke
Jn./John
Acts/Acts of the Apostles
Rom./Romans
1 Cor./1 Corinthians
2 Cor./2 Corinthians
Gal./Galatians
Eph./Ephesians
Phil./Philippians
Col./Colossians
1 Thess./1 Thessalonians
2 Thess./2 Thessalonians
1 Tim./1 Timothy
2 Tim./2 Timothy
Tit./Titus
Philem./Philemon

Heb./Hebrews
Jas./James
1 Pet./1 Peter
2 Pet./2 Peter
1 Jn./1 John
2 Jn./2 John
3 Jn./3 John
Jude/Jude
Rev./Revelation (Apocalypse)

# INTRODUCTION

The Council of Jerusalem constitutes a central turning point in the Acts of the Apostles (cf. Acts 15). The practice of baptizing Gentiles without prior circumcision had earlier been initiated by Peter and confirmed by the Jerusalem church (cf. Acts 10–11). The Council of Jerusalem further determined that such Gentiles did not need subsequently to be circumcised and follow the Deuteronomic Law.[1] The Council thereby confirmed the mission to the Gentiles, which Paul promptly set out to pursue to the fullest.

The proponents of the Gentile mission were impelled by their vision of covenantal history, beginning with the covenants of the Old Testament and culminating in the Messianic work of their own day. In His oath to Abraham, God had promised blessing for all the nations (Gen. 22:16–18). Yet, by the time of the first century, it had become difficult to see how God's blessing could come even to Israel, much less to all the nations. Of the twelve tribes descended from Abraham, Isaac, and Jacob, the ten northern tribes had been completely scattered among the Gentiles. The kingdom of Judah, ruled by the house of David, had then been destroyed, partially scattering the two southern tribes.

---

[1] Stephen Pimentel, *Witnesses of the Messiah: On Acts of Apostles 1–15* (Steubenville, OH: Emmaus Road Publishing, 2002), 127–140.

Nevertheless, the great hope of Israel, proclaimed by the Old Testament prophets, centered on the restoration of the kingdom, understood not merely as a political entity encompassing a single nation, but as God's rule on earth spreading to all the nations. In accordance with the Father's economy of salvation, Jesus the Messiah had fulfilled the prophecies and inaugurated the promised kingdom. Israel must now undergo a New Exodus in which all twelve of her tribes would be regathered into the restored kingdom. The evangelization of the Gentiles would be instrumental to this restoration because most of the Israelites were scattered among them. Paul understood his own mission as precisely this prophetic regathering of the twelve tribes through the evangelization of the Gentiles (cf. Acts 26:6–7).

The restored kingdom had been inaugurated through a New Covenant that fulfilled God's promise to Abraham. Thus, the kingdom was open to all who would enter the New Covenant, regardless of physical descent. The New Covenant did not create a "second" People of God alongside Israel, but encompassed all in Israel who would received the Holy Spirit.[2] Paul's mission to the nations sought to bring within the New Covenant all who would accept the Good News of the kingdom, which would attain its final culmination on earth with the resurrection of the dead. Until that great resurrection, the Messiah must reign in the presence of enemies (cf. 1 Cor. 15:23–25), who

---

[2] See Second Vatican Council, Dogmatic Constitution on the Church *Lumen Gentium* (November 21, 1964), no. 9; *Catechism*, no. 781.

are brought into submission only through the evangelization of the nations.

When the resurrection of the dead might occur was a mystery, but the apostles knew that Jesus had prophesied the destruction of Jerusalem and its temple within "this generation" (Lk. 21:32). Paul pursued his mission during the period of covenantal transition between the death of Jesus and the destruction of the temple, a new period of forty years in the wilderness like that of the generation of Israelites led by Moses in the wilderness (see Acts 7:36, 42; 13:18; 1 Cor. 10:1–11). Like Peter, Paul carried out his ministry in the shadow of Jesus' prophecy, preaching salvation from "this crooked generation" (Acts 2:40). The coming destruction of the temple would entail the visible end of the sacrificial cult at the heart of the Deuteronomic covenant and so complete the transition to the New Covenant. Paul was desperate to save every Israelite whom he might reach, including those scattered among the Gentiles (cf. Rom. 9:2–3; 11:25–26). In the face of fierce resistance and persecution, he ceaselessly proclaimed the lordship of Jesus, calling all to the baptismal gift of the Spirit and the Eucharistic kingdom of the twelve tribes (cf. Lk. 22:28–30).

## Second Journey
### —Acts 16—

After the Council of Jerusalem, Paul and Barnabas accompanied Judas and Silas, the delegates chosen by the Council, on their way to Antioch (Acts 15:22–23, 30). After delivering the decrees of the Council to that city, Paul and Silas proceeded on to the churches of Syria and Cilicia (Acts 15:41), delivering "for observance the decisions (*dogmata*) which had been reached by the apostles and elders who were at Jerusalem" (Acts 16:4). In the nearby city of Lystra, they were joined by Timothy, "the son of a Jewish woman" (Acts 16:1) who had probably become a disciple during the earlier journey of Paul and Barnabas (cf. Acts 14:6–7). Although Timothy's father was a Gentile, he would have been considered a Jew by other Jews on account of his mother, albeit one who was living in violation of the Deuteronomic Law due to his lack of circumcision. Paul therefore circumcised Timothy to avoid giving scandal to other Jews, in accordance with his customary policy: "to the Jews I became as a Jew, in order to win Jews; to those under the law I became as one under the law—though not being myself under the law—that I might win those under the law" (1 Cor. 9:20).[1]

---

[1] In contrast, Paul strenuously refused to circumcise Titus because the latter was a Gentile on whom the Deuteronomic Law had no claim (cf. Gal. 2:3–5). For further discussion of the status of the Law in relation to Jewish and Gentile disciples during this period, see Pimentel, *Witnesses of the Messiah*, 127–29.

The missionaries continued to extend the kingdom of Christ by building up His Church throughout the region (Acts 16:5). At this point in the narrative, the Holy Spirit acts to guide the mission of evangelization, apparently through the providential ordering of circumstances. Luke reports that, while in the Galatia, the missionaries were "forbidden by the Holy Spirit" to go west to the province of Asia. Paul, in his letter to the Galatians, states that "it was because of a bodily ailment that I preached the gospel to you" (Gal. 4:13). They next attempted to go north to Bithynia, but again "the Spirit of Jesus did not allow them" (Acts 16:7). Luke's language reflects his understanding that the Holy Spirit never acts apart from Jesus but always carries out the mission of the latter.

The missionaries took the one remaining direction in which they could press forward and headed northwest to Troas (Acts 16:8), the region in which ancient Troy had stood. It is in Troas that the party was apparently joined by Luke himself.[2] Once they were in Troas, the Holy Spirit intervened in their itinerary in a more dramatic fashion. Paul received a vision "in the night," probably in a dream, of a Macedonian begging the party to come to Macedonia to "help us" (Acts 16:9). They immediately grasped that the "help" needed was the proclamation of the Gospel (Acts 16:10), for the liberation brought by the

---

[2] The first "we" section in Acts, in which Luke employs the first-person plural, begins in Acts 16:10 and extends through Acts 16:17. See Stanley E. Porter, *Paul in Acts*, ed. Stanley E. Porter, Library of Pauline Studies (Peabody, MA: Hendrickson Publishers, 2001), 28–29. Luke apparently remained in Philippi when Paul and Silas departed (Acts 16:40).

Gospel is desperately needed by persons and cultures held in bondage by the powers of sin.

The missionaries thus set sail across the Aegean to Macedonia, the province north of Greece (Acts 16:11). By this westward voyage, the mission of evangelization pressed on toward "the end of the earth" in fulfillment of Jesus' command (Acts 1:8). They soon came to Philippi, an important Macedonian city that lay along the major road between Rome and Byzantium and which had been given the status of a Roman "colony" (*kolonia*) by Augustus Caesar. As such, Philippi served as a retirement location for veterans of the Roman army, and most of its inhabitants were Roman citizens.

### The Lydian Woman

There were few Jews in Philippi, apparently too few to support a formal synagogue,[3] so the missionaries sought out the informal "place of prayer" (*proseuche*) where Jews and Gentile "God-fearers" gathered on the Sabbath. There, they encountered Lydia, one of the Gentile God-fearers in whom the Gospel quickly took root. The name "Lydia" is not a proper Greek or Roman name, but a place name literally meaning "the Lydian woman."[4] Such a name indicates that Lydia was a former slave who was so named by her master. Luke does not indicate how long Lydia had been free but simply identifies her as a "seller of purple goods" (Acts 16:14). Textile

---

[3] The establishment of a synagogue required at least ten Jewish households headed by adult men.

[4] Lydia was a province in Asia Minor.

work was typically performed by slaves, and Lydia may well have gone into business in the line of work she had learned before her emancipation. In any case, she was now known by her profession, suggesting that she had become quite successful in that business.[5]

When Lydia heard Paul's proclamation of the Gospel, the Holy Spirit "opened her heart" (Acts 16:14) to receive it, drawing her toward the New Covenant.[6] Lydia thereby becomes a type of Gentile acceptance of the Word of God. No sooner had Lydia been baptized than she undertook her apostolate, beginning with the conversion of her own household and immediately turning to the missionaries, to whom she extended that sacred hospitality (*philoxenia*) that was so highly valued in the ancient world (cf. Acts 16:15). Suffused with the theological virtue of charity, her hospitality expresses gratitude not only to her human benefactors but, more profoundly, to the Word. The ultimate meaning of her hospitality is thus acceptance of Christ in the person of the befriended stranger (*xenos*). Although Jews, Paul and Silas did not refuse to stay at the house of this Gentile woman.[7]

---

[5] Marie-Eloise Rosenblatt, *Paul the Accused: His Portrait in the Acts of the Apostles*, ed. Mary Ann Getty, Zacchaeus Studies: New Testament (Collegeville, MN: Michael Glazier, The Liturgical Press, 1995), 46–47.

[6] Paul elaborates on the renewal of the heart within the New Covenant in 2 Cor. 3:2–3, drawing on the prophecies of the New Covenant in Jer. 31:31 and Ezek. 36:26.

[7] In contrast, Peter is willing to enter the house of the Gentile Cornelius only after receiving a vision followed by explicit instruction from the Holy Spirit to accompany Cornelius' emissaries "without hesitation" (cf. Acts 10:10–29). See Pimentel, *Witnesses of the Messiah*, 98–101.

## A Girl Enslaved

On the way to the place of prayer, the missionaries encountered a girl who, unlike Lydia, is still enslaved. Even more, the girl was enslaved not only to human masters but to a demonic power. She is said to have "a spirit of divination" or, more literally, "a Pythonic spirit" (Acts 16:16). The Python was the serpent whose spirit was believed by the Greeks to inhabit the temple of Apollo at Delphi. This spirit would possess the priestess of Apollo and speak oracles through her. Thus, Luke understands a "Pythonic spirit" to be a demon under whose influence one engages in divination. The demon also performed a second function, closely linked to the first, bringing the slave owners "much gain by soothsaying." The provision of material wealth is one of the perennial temptations by which the demons seek to entice men, eventually ensnaring them in a bondage both spiritual and material. Such multifaceted enslavement was a defining characteristic of the pagan world.

The girl followed the missionaries, shouting: "These men are servants of the Most High God, who proclaim to you the way of salvation" (Acts 16:17). The demons know well the truths of the spiritual realm (cf. Lk. 4:34), and will often speak them amidst their lies in order to confuse those attracted by the Gospel. The slave owners apparently saw the attention that the missionaries were receiving through the proclamation of the Gospel and sought to exploit the gathered crowds, following the missionaries about so as to market the girl's power of divination. At first, the missionaries ignored the evil hucksters, but after "many days" of interference and distraction, Paul finally turned and cast the demon out of the girl (Acts 16:18), just as Jesus had often done (cf. Lk. 4:35). The power of the Gospel, spread through human cultures by evangelization, progressively breaks the power of demonic influence over those cultures.

### The Slave Owners

The exorcism provoked a sharp reaction from the slave owners, leading to Paul's first conflict with Gentiles during the course of his evangelization. Dismayed by the loss of their source of wealth, the slave owners "seized Paul and Silas" and "brought them to the magistrates" (Acts 16:19–20). In their hostile response to Paul, these Gentiles show themselves to be the spiritual antithesis of Lydia, rejecting rather than accepting Christ in the person of the stranger. Hereafter, Paul's relations with Gentiles will be marked by this bifurcating pattern of acceptance or rejection, depending on his audience's receptivity to the Word of God.

The slave owners charged Paul and Silas with advocating customs unlawful for Romans (Acts 16:21). While seemingly unrelated to the preceding events, this charge actually has a subtle connection to the slave owner's loss of a demonically enabled stream of wealth. The pagan religious ethos, with its polytheism and idolatry, was embraced and institutionalized in Roman law, and that ethos was one in which demonic influence flourished. It is not coincidental that the slave owners begin their complaint with the fact that "these men are Jews" (Acts 16:20), known opponents of polytheism and idolatry. In an ironic sense that the slave owners themselves may not fully grasp, their charge against the missionaries is true. The lordship of Jesus Christ proclaimed in the Gospel is universal in scope and subordinates all other claims.[8] As Paul will later write to the Philippians, "at the name of Jesus every knee should bow, in heaven and on earth and under the earth, and every tongue confess that Jesus Christ is Lord" (Phil. 2:10–11). If Jesus is now Lord of all, then neither Satan nor Caesar can be accorded that honor, as much as the pagan ethos sought to bestow it on them. Hence, the Gospel truly was contrary to the prevailing customs of the Romans.

## The Philippian Jailer

The magistrates ordered Paul and Silas to be beaten and handed over to the city jailer for imprisonment (Acts 16:22–24). The jailer dutifully secured his charges with fetters in the prison, only to have his work suddenly undone by "a great earthquake" that unlocked all the doors and fetters therein (Acts 16:24–26). Fearing the escape of the prisoners, the jailer prepared to kill himself to avoid the consequent loss of honor and impending punishment, only to be stopped by Paul's declaration that no one has taken advantage of the earthquake by fleeing (Acts 16:27–28). Having been saved from the circumstance that threatened his physical life, the jailer turned in

---

[8] N. T. Wright, *What Saint Paul Really Said: Was Paul of Tarsus the Real Founder of Christianity?* (Grand Rapids: William B. Eerdmans Publishing Company, 1997), 56–57.

gratitude and sought the missionaries' word concerning his spiritual life: "Men, what must I do to be
saved?" (Acts 16:29–30). They proclaimed to him the
necessity of faith in Jesus (Acts 16:31–32), a faith that
will lead him to be baptized that very day. At once,
the jailer offered hospitality to the missionaries,
beginning by washing their wounded bodies. They in
turn wash his soul in the waters of Baptism, along
"with all his family" (Acts 16:33). Paul taught that
Baptism is the sign of the New Covenant, just as circumcision was for the Abrahamic covenant (cf. Col.
2:11–12). The necessity of circumcision applied, without regard to age, to an entire household living within the Abrahamic covenant.[9] In the cases of both
Lydia and the jailer, Baptism is treated according to
the same covenantal pattern.

The jailer continued his hospitality by receiving
the missionaries in his house and serving them a meal
(Acts 16:34). The transformation of his relationship
with the missionaries is now complete. The man who
began as their jailer has now become their host.
Whereas Lydia is a type of the ready acceptance of
Christ and the slave owners of rejection, the
Philippian jailer moves from a stance of rejection to
one of acceptance, becoming a type of conversion. The
change in his interior relation to Christ is reflected in
his exterior actions toward the strangers who came in
His name.

---

[9] The precise requirement was that any male, eight days old or older,
regardless of status within the household, must be circumcised (see
Gen. 17:12–13).

## The Vindication of the Evangelist

Unaware of the events that transpired after the missionaries' imprisonment, the magistrates judged their punishment to be sufficient and ordered them released (Acts 16:35–36). Paul, however, refused to let the matter pass so easily. He had been publicly subjected to a beating, a punishment considered dishonorable and from which Roman citizens were exempt. Accordingly, he insisted that his vindication by the authorities be public as well (Acts 16:37). Provincial magistrates were required to uphold the rights of Roman citizens and so, when they heard of Paul's citizenship and insistence on the rights thereof, "they were afraid" (Acts 16:38). They therefore apologized to Paul and Silas and escorted them out of the prison themselves. The missionaries' situation among the Gentiles has undergone a reversal, moving from rejection and imprisonment to acceptance and release. After visiting Lydia and the new disciples, Paul and Silas departed Philippi, probably leaving Luke behind to further guide the nascent Church. In the years to come, Paul experienced few problems with the Philippian church, and it served as a major source of financial support for his missions (cf. Phil. 4:15).

\*　　\*　　\*

## Questions for Discussion

**1.** Read Acts 16:3. In what ways should we take care not to offend others unnecessarily in our presentation of the Catholic faith?

_____

_____

_____

_____

_____

_____

**2.** Read Acts 16:4. Do we strive in our apostolate to convey accurately and completely the teachings of the Magisterium?

_____

_____

_____

_____

_____

_____

**3.** Read Acts 16:15. What role should the exercise of hospitality play in our apostolates?

_____

_____

_____

_____

_____

# 2

## AMONG THE GREEKS
### —ACTS 17—

From Philippi, Paul and Silas traveled to Thessalonica (Acts 17:1), the capital of the Roman province of Macedonia. Unlike Philippi, Thessalonica had a Jewish population sufficiently large to support a synagogue, in which Paul immediately began to evangelize. There, he "argued" (*dielexato*) or reasoned with the Jews "from the scriptures" (Acts 17:2). In other words, Paul's evangelization took the form of an explanation of the Gospel from the prophetic texts of the Old Testament. He did not chiefly seek to demonstrate that "the Christ," or royal successor of David, had been promised by the prophets, for such was commonly believed among first-century Jews. Rather, he sought to demonstrate something far more challenging to his audience, "that it was necessary for the Christ to suffer and to rise from the dead" (Acts 17:3; cf. 1 Cor 15:3–4).[1] On the basis of these Messianic characteristics, Paul could then argue that "this Jesus, whom I proclaim to you, is the Christ" (Acts 17:3).

### Persecution in Thessalonica

Some of the Jews to whom Paul preached accepted the message of the Gospel, as did even more of the Gentile proselytes (Acts 17:4). Other Jews, however,

---

[1] Luke, in his account of the sermon at Pisidian Antioch (Acts 13:26–31), gives a more detailed example of Paul's use of the Old Testament to explain the death and Resurrection of the Messiah. See Pimentel, *Witnesses of the Messiah*, 117–120.

"were jealous" of the missionaries' success (Acts 17:5), leading to the most persistent persecution experienced by Paul's converts in Greece or Macedonia. In Philippi, Paul and Silas had been arrested, beaten, and imprisoned (Acts 16:19–24), but this was instigated by disgruntled slave owners (Acts 16:16–18) rather than being a broadly support-ed persecution. In Corinth, Paul would be brought before the tribunal by some local Jews (Acts 18:12–16), but the charges were quickly dismissed. In Thessalonica, on the other hand, Paul's oppo-nents organized a mob in an attempt to lynch him (Acts 17:5). Failing to find him, they then "dragged" his converts "before the city authorities" to press charges against them (Acts 17:6).

The missionaries were charged with claiming that there is "another king," Jesus, the same charges brought against Jesus Himself (cf. Lk. 23:2). This charge relates back to Paul's proclamation in verse 3 of Jesus as "the Christ." "King" (*basileus*) was the title given to the emperor in the Greek-speaking part of the empire. Thus, to declare allegiance to "another" king was considered treasonous. To understand the logic behind this charge, one must grasp the role of civil religion within the Roman empire. The emperor did not claim only to be a secular political ruler. In fact, the idea of "secular politics" did not exist in the ancient world, whether among the Gentiles or Jews. Rather, like all Hellenistic monarchs, the emperor claimed to rule on behalf of the gods. To confess Jesus as Lord is necessarily to reject that claim. Thus, the proclamation of Jesus as Lord contradicted the civil religion that served as the foundation of the emperor's sovereignty.[2] Paul taught the Thessalonians that Jesus is the true King, reigning now in heaven, from which He will come to judge all (cf. 1 Thess. 4:15–17). Paul did not deny that the emperor was, in fact, the emperor and as such was to be obeyed. He simply asserted that the emperor, like all earthly authorities, received his authority from the true God, not from Jupiter or Zeus (cf. Rom. 13:1–5).

## The Noble Jews of Beroea

The Thessalonian city authorities were sufficiently "disturbed" by the charge against the missionaries to require "security" to be paid on their behalf by the disciples before releasing the latter (Acts 17:8–9). Not waiting for their persecutors to find Paul and Silas, the disciples then sent them "away by night to Beroea," a neighboring Macedonian city (Acts 17:10). Once more in the drama of evangelization, divine providence employed opposition to the Gospel to further its spread, for in the synagogue of Beroea, the missionaries' message would find a more a favorable reception. In Luke's famous description of the Beroean Jews, "they received the word with all eagerness, examining the scriptures daily to see if these things were so" (Acts 17:11). The scriptures that the Beroeans examined to test the Gospel were those of the Old Testament, and the result of their diligent study was that "many of them therefore believed" (Acts 17:12). The experience of the Beroean Jews exemplifies the centrality of the Old Testament to the proclamation and interpretation of the Gospel.

---

[2] Wright, *What Saint Paul Really Said*, 52–53, 149.

However, the newly founded church of Beroea was not to remain at peace. The Jews of Thessalonica discovered that Paul had gone to Beroea after fleeing their own city. In a remarkable display of perseverance in hostility, they then pursued Paul to Beroea, renewing the persecution and forcing him to flee yet again (Acts 17:13–14). Such determination suggests that the opposition among the Thessalonian Jews to Paul's mission was both intense and sustained. In his letters to the Thessalonian disciples, Paul would refer to their subsequent experience of persecution (see 1 Thess. 2:14, 3:3–4; 2 Thess. 1:4). Opposition to the Gospel intensified even as the kingdom of God advanced, like the weeds that grow in the field along with wheat (Mt. 13:24–30).

Seeking to protect Paul from his Thessalonian persecutors, the disciples of Beroea sent him on to Athens (Acts 17:15). While in Athens, Paul was "provoked" by the pronounced idolatry within the city, motivating his subsequent preaching among the Athenians (Acts 17:16–17). In accordance with the prophetic teaching of the Old Testament, Paul understood such idolatry to be demonic in origin (cf. 1 Cor. 10:20).

### The Philosophers of Athens

In addition to his usual practice of preaching to the Jews and proselytes in the synagogue, Paul also debated with the Epicurean and Stoic philosophers in the marketplace, proclaiming "Jesus and the resurrection" (Acts 17:17–18). This "new teaching" struck the philosophers as "strange," and so they invited Paul to explain his teaching further before the

Areopagus, the council of the learned that met on the Hill of Ares (Acts 17:19–20).

Paul's discourse before the Areopagus is his longest to a Gentile audience recorded in the Book of Acts. In this discourse, Paul employs a strategy of "polemical engagement" with Greek philosophy, adverting to its concepts while redirecting them toward the Gospel.[3] At the same time, Paul's thought remains anchored in Scripture. Though never quoting the Old Testament, Paul's terminology in the discourse is drawn directly from the Pentateuch.

Paul begins by noting how "very religious" (*deisidai-monesterous*) the Athenians are (Acts 17:22). This term (literally, "greatly fearing gods") is ambiguous, having negative as well as positive connotations. From a biblical perspective, most "religion" in the ancient world was polytheistic, idolatrous, and closely linked to immorality. Although Paul does not emphasize the connection with immorality in this discourse,[4] he does draw attention to the problem of idolatry.

## Creator and Creation

Without mentioning the distress he had experienced, Paul then relates his tour of the shrines, altar, and idols of Athens. He takes as his point of theological departure an altar dedicated "to an unknown god" (Acts 17:23). With more than a little irony, Paul declares that the one deity of the Athenians whom he is willing to endorse is the one whom they admit they

---

[3] Wright, *What Saint Paul Really Said*, 80–81.
[4] In contrast, Rom. 1:23–25 stresses the relation between idolatry and immorality.

do not know. This God, Paul proclaims, is none other than the Creator of "the world and everything in it" (Acts 17:24). As does the Book of Genesis, Paul begins his explanation with God's role as Creator.

As the Creator of all things, God transcends His creation. Thus, Paul clearly marks the distinction between Creator and creation, in contrast to Stoic pantheism.[5] The creation is contingent and dependent on the Creator; it is not itself divine. However, Paul is not content to leave this observation at the merely philosophic level, but immediately draws its practical implication for worship: the transcendent God does not live in shrines "made by man" (*cheiropoietos*) (Acts 17:24). The term *cheiropoietos* is used throughout the Greek Old Testament exclusively in reference to pagan idols.[6] Failure to recognize and honor the transcendence of God is a chief source of idolatry (cf. Rom. 1:21–23).

Paul then briefly summarizes the doctrine of Genesis 1–11, focusing on the unity of the human race and God's providence over human history, including that of the Gentiles (cf. Acts 17:26).[7] The purpose of God's providence is that men "should seek God, in the hope that they might feel after him and find him" (Acts 17:27). Paul thus encapsulates the root intuition behind all authentic philosophic reflection. The possibility of attaining knowledge of God rests on His presence within creation (cf. Rom.

---

[5] Porter, *Paul in Acts*, 120.
[6] Saint Stephen uses the same term in Acts 7:47–48 to suggest that his audience held an idolatrous attitude toward the Jerusalem temple. See Pimentel, *Witnesses of the Messiah*, 76.
[7] Paul's language echoes a similar summary in Deut. 32:8.

1:19–20), an insight consonant with Stoicism but contrary to Epicureanism.

However, men are not only creatures of God but also His children (Acts 17:28), created in His "image" and after His "likeness" (Gen. 1:26–27). Due to the spiritual character of his own nature, man has the capacity to know God not only through reflection on the created world (*Catechism*, no. 32, 36) but also through reflection on himself (*Catechism*, no. 33). If man is the child of God, then God must not be treated as a creature fashioned or manipulated by man. The Greek philosophers grasped this point, but they were unwilling to draw the logical conclusion that idolatry should therefore be eschewed (cf. Acts 17:29). Such a moral error will prove catastrophic in its consequences, as God "has fixed a day on which he will judge the world in righteousness" (Acts 17:31; cf. Rom. 1:18).

## The Resurrected Christ

Here, at the end of the discourse, Paul introduces the revelation of the New Covenant. The judgment of the world will be carried out by Christ, whose Resurrection was the greatest contingent event in the history of mankind. The orientation of much Greek philosophy, with its search for universal principles of order, was resistant to according ultimate significance to any contingent historical event. Nevertheless, Paul declares, in and through this one man and event, God has chosen to reveal Himself. The Resurrection is thus God's "assurance" of the Gospel, given "to all" (Acts 17:31) so that the Gospel may be genuinely catholic, destined for every nation and ethnicity.

In response to Paul's proclamation of the resurrection of the dead, some of the philosophers "mocked" him (Acts 17:32). The doctrine of the general resurrection, with its affirmation of the enduring value of the body, stood in strong tension with the various schools of Greek philosophy and would prove among the Greeks to be a major point of resistance to which Paul would have to respond (cf. 1 Cor. 15:12–56). The mockery of the Athenian philosophers reflected an attitude of rationalistic unbelief for which the Gospel can only appear as foolishness (cf. 1 Cor. 1:18–25). It is noteworthy that Paul had greater success in establishing churches throughout Macedonia, where he was harshly persecuted, than in Athens, where the learned cared no more than to mock him.

\*   \*   \*

## Questions for Discussion

**1.** Read Acts 17:5,13,32. In what ways is the Gospel opposed in contemporary America? Does this opposition more closely resemble that of the Thessalonians or the Athenians?

_____

_____

_____

_____

_____

_____

How should we respond when our witness to Christ is opposed?

_____

_____

_____

_____

**2.** Read Acts 17:22–29. In our own apostolates, how can we engage with contemporary thought while redirecting it toward the Gospel? How does Divine Revelation, as given in Scripture and Tradition, serve as a guide for such engagement?

_____

_____

_____

_____

_____

_____

**3.** Read Acts 17:18, 21, 32. What forms of rationalistic unbelief do we encounter today? Do we see combinations of novelty-seeking and skepticism similar to those of the Athenians?

_____

_____

_____

_____

_____

_____

# 3

## RETURNING HOME
### —ACTS 18—

From Athens, Paul traveled to Corinth, which the Romans had made the capital of the province of Achaia (Acts 18:1). Paul would later write that he arrived in Corinth "in weakness and in much fear and trembling" due to the persecution and rejection that he had previously encountered in Macedonia and Achaia. Upon arriving in the city, Paul found that he was preceded by Aquila and Priscilla, disciples from the Jewish community in Rome.[1] The emperor Claudius is known to have expelled the Jews from Rome in AD 49, probably due to strife in the synagogues between those who accepted and those who rejected Christ (see Acts 18:2). Like Paul, Aquila and Priscilla were tentmakers, and for a time they went into business together (Acts 18:3). By practicing such a profession, Paul was able to avoid reliance on patronage (1 Cor. 9:12, 15–18), while reaching the many people who came to the city's market.[2] Every sabbath, Paul would leave the market and go to the synagogue to evangelize the Jews and Greek proselytes (Acts 18:4; 1 Cor. 1:22–24, 9:20–21). Silas and Timothy found Paul thus occupied when they arrived from Macedonia (Acts 18:5).

---

[1] Aquila and Priscilla later served the church in Ephesus (1 Cor. 16:19) before returning to Rome (Rom. 16:3).

[2] Ben Witherington III, *The Paul Quest: The Renewed Search for the Jew of Tarsus* (Downers Grove, IL: InterVarsity Press, 1998), 129.

## The Word of the Prophet

Eventually, however, a number of the Jews began heatedly to oppose Paul's evangelism, making him no longer welcome in the synagogue. He therefore announced that he would henceforth go to the Gentiles of Corinth, just as he had earlier done in Pisidian Antioch when faced with similar rejection (Acts 13:46).[3] In a prophetic gesture of judgment, Paul "shook out his garments" before the synagogue (cf. Neh. 5:13) and declared, "Your blood be upon your heads!" (Acts 18:6). The reference to their "blood" echoes the language of Ezekiel's prophetic call (cf. Ezek. 3:17–21). With the destruction of Jerusalem pending, God charged Ezekiel to convey His message of repentance to Israel, warning the prophet that if he failed to do so, he would be responsible for the "blood" of those who failed to repent.[4] Paul's declaration to his opponents indicates that he, like a good prophet, has faithfully conveyed the Good News of the Messiah to Israel. He is therefore not responsible for the temporal and spiritual consequences of their rejection of God's Word.

Having been blocked from evangelizing within the synagogue itself, Paul shifted to the house next door, which was owned by a sympathetic Gentile proselyte (Acts 18:7). From his new location, Paul met with considerable success evangelizing both Jews and Gentiles, ironically including Crispus, one of the synagogue

---

[3] Pimentel, *Witnesses of the Messiah*, 122.
[4] Ezekiel received his call in 593 BC, and Jerusalem was destroyed several years later in 586 BC. See Willem A. VanGemeren, *Interpreting the Prophetic Word: An Introduction to the Prophetic Literature of the Old Testament* (Grand Rapids: Zondervan Publishing House, 1990), 323.

elders (Acts 18:8).[5] Yet, in spite of his success, Paul must have been concerned for his own safety, given the persecution he had previously experienced. As if in response to such concerns, the Lord Jesus, who had appeared to Paul on the road to Damascus (Acts 9:5), now appeared to him in Corinth and uttered the very words by which the prophets Isaiah and Jeremiah had been strengthened: "Do not be afraid, . . . for I am with you" (cf. Is. 41:10; Jer. 1:8). With regard to evangelizing the Corinthians, Paul must "speak and . . . not be silent; . . . and no man shall attack you," in contrast to Paul's experience in the other cities. The Lord knew that "many people in this city" would respond to Paul's proclamation of the Gospel, so he should remain in Corinth and continue evangelizing (Acts 18:9–10). In obedience to this instruction, Paul remained in Corinth for "a year and six months" (Acts 18:11).

## The Rule of Law

At some point during this period, the Jews who had opposed Paul in the synagogue "made a united attack" on him, bringing him before the proconsul Gallio (Acts 18:12)[6] and charging him with "persuading men to worship God contrary to the law" (Acts 18:13). The law that Paul is accused of violating is the

---

[5] Crispus was one of the few Corinthians whom Paul personally baptized (1 Cor. 1:14).

[6] Gallio, the brother of the Stoic philosopher and tragedian Lucius Seneca, was proconsul of Achaia from AD 51 to 52. See Simon Hornblower and Antony Spawforth, eds. *The Oxford Classical Dictionary*, 3d ed. (Oxford; New York: Oxford University Press, 1996), 95–98.

Mosaic Law, in accordance with which the Jews were officially permitted to govern their own communities within the Roman empire. Paul's opponents were attempting to give a subversive political import to deviation from the Mosaic Law, arguing that, by promoting a deviant system of worship, Paul was promulgating a different religion not permitted by Roman law.

Gallio, however, quickly cut off this line of argument and dismissed the charges against Paul (Acts 18:14). He saw the dispute as clearly pertaining to "your own law," i.e., the Mosaic Law, concerning whose precepts he refused to "be a judge." By commanding the parties to the dispute to "see to it yourselves," he effectively declared that Roman law would, for the time being, view the worship of Christ as having the same legal status as Judaism. Gallio's only concern was to uphold the rule of law and the *Pax Romana* that it served, not for the "words and names" of the God of Israel. Such an attitude undoubtedly appeared to be the way of prudence for a Roman proconsul dealing with unruly provincials. However, the servants of the empire would soon enough learn that Christ is a sign of contradiction for Gentile and Jew alike, and they would have no choice but to care for "these things" (Acts 18:15).

Gallio sent the Jews away from the tribunal, whereupon they vented their rage on Sosthenes, another synagogue elder who had accepted the Gospel (Acts 18:16–17; cf. 1 Cor. 1:1). Nevertheless, the overall outcome of the conflict was favorable for Paul. For the first time during his journey, he was not obliged to leave the city after a legal confrontation, but was free to remain in Corinth for "many days longer" (Acts 18:18).

## Back to Antioch

Eventually, Paul departed Corinth with Aquila and Priscilla, leaving Timothy and Silas to tend the Corinthian church. The party stopped at Ephesus in the province of Asia, which Paul had been prevented from entering prior to crossing into Macedonia (Acts 16:6). On the present occasion, Paul spent only a short time in Ephesus, although the city would become a focal point of his third journey. Aquila and Priscilla remained behind in Ephesus to evangelize, while Paul continued sailing eastward (Acts 18:19–21). He soon landed at Caesarea, the port used when traveling to Jerusalem by sea. Paul briefly visited Jerusalem before returning to his home base of Antioch, in which he remained for "some time" (Acts 18:22–23).

\* \* \*

## Questions for Discussion

**1.** Read Acts 18:2–3, 18–19 and Rom. 16:3–5. How did Aquila and Priscilla engage in the apostolate? What sacrifices did they probably make to do so?

_____

_____

_____

_____

How can the laity most effectively engage in the apostolate today?

_____

_____

_____

_____

**2.** Read Acts 18:9–10. How do we respond to God's call to "speak and . . . not be silent" in the apostolate? How do we attempt to seek the "many people in this city" who would respond to the Gospel?

_____

_____

_____

_____

**3.** Read Acts 18:14–15 and the *Catechism*, no. 1910. From a Catholic perspective, how was Gallio's exclusive concern for public order deficient?

_____

_____

_____

_____

How should Catholic public officials seek to promote the common good? In what areas is the promotion of the common good most contentious today?

_____

_____

_____

_____

## 4

# THIRD JOURNEY
## —ACTS 18—

Paul began his third missionary journey in AD
53, leaving Antioch and proceeding through the
area he had earlier evangelized around Galatia
and Phrygia (Acts 18:23). Traveling westward, he
eventually arrived at Ephesus (Acts 19:1), the leading
city in the province of Asia. Upon arriving at Ephesus,
Paul encountered a group of disciples of John the
Baptist. Paul questioned them and determined that
they had not yet been baptized into the Body of Christ
nor received the Holy Spirit (Acts 19:2–3). He therefore instructed them concerning the relationship
between John the Baptist and Christ (Acts 19:4), para-
phrasing John's own self-description: "John answered
them all, 'I baptize you with water; but he who is
mightier than I is coming, the thong of whose sandals
I am not worthy to untie; he will baptize you with the
Holy Spirit and with fire'" (Lk. 3:16). Hence, Paul
stressed that the baptism of John was not the sacra-
mental Baptism of the New Covenant, but only a
preparation for it.

Upon receiving Paul's instruction, the disciples of
John accepted their need for Baptism and
Confirmation. Luke refers to their Baptism "in the
name of the Lord Jesus" to distinguish such from the
preparatory baptism of John (Acts 19:5). Immediately
after their Baptism, Paul administered the sacrament
of Confirmation through the laying on of hands,
thereby bestowing the Holy Spirit (cf. Acts 19:6). In
this way, the disciples of John the Baptist at Ephesus

were received into union with the Church, confessing "one Lord, one faith, one baptism"(Eph. 4:5).

Following his usual practice, Paul began his evangelization of Ephesus in the synagogue, "arguing" that, with the Resurrection of Jesus, the Messianic "kingdom of God" was now unfolding (Acts 19:8). This initial phase of his ministry continued for three months, until he was compelled by the opposition of some of the Jews to abandon the synagogue for a nearby hall (Acts 19:9). In Hellenistic culture, a "hall" or "school" (*schole*) was a place used for instruction in arts such as rhetoric or philosophy. For the next two years, Paul used this hall as a base for his evangelization, proclaiming the Gospel to the residents of the entire province of Asia (Acts 19:10).

## The Name of the Lord Jesus

The Ephesians were known for their cultivation of occult practices, so much so that "magical words" were called *Ephesia grammata*.[1] These practices included the attempt to manipulate demons, whether to exorcise them from the possessed or to harness their power for the casting of spells. It may have been to overcome such practices that the Holy Spirit endowed Paul's ministry in Ephesus with extraordinary manifestations of divine power. Articles of clothing that Paul had worn were used by the disciples to heal the sick and to perform exorcisms (Acts 19:11–12). The reputation of Paul's ministry grew to

---

[1] Georg Luck, *Arcana Mundi: Magic and the Occult in the Greek and Roman Worlds* (Baltimore: The Johns Hopkins University Press, 1985), 17.

the point that "itinerant Jewish exorcists" who had not accepted the Gospel nevertheless began "to pronounce the name of the Lord Jesus" in their own attempted exorcisms (Acts 19:13). Reflecting a popular superstition according to which the invocation of a deity's name gave one access to the power of that deity, these exorcists were quite willing to invoke the name of one whom they did not accept as Lord. However, they quickly discovered that the name of Jesus has power only when invoked with genuine faith in Him. As they attempted to cast out a demon, it responded to their abuse of Jesus' name with the dismissive rebuke, "Jesus I know, and Paul I know, but who are you?" (Acts 19:15-16).

Thus, the "residents of Ephesus, both Jews and Greeks," saw that Christ was victorious over both the demons and those who would seek to manipulate the latter. They thereby learned that the power of the Gospel, however extraordinary its manifestations, is not equivalent to any kind of magic. In consequence, "fear fell upon them all; and the name of the Lord Jesus was extolled" (Acts 19:17). A properly motivated fear can be a spur to further conversion (see Prov. 1:7), and so it proved in Ephesus, as the new disciples renounced their practice of "magic arts" (Acts 19:18-19). Many of the new disciples publicly burned their books of magic spells in spite of their great monetary value so as to give public witness that "the word of the Lord" had "prevailed" over the occult powers (Acts 19:19-20). As the kingdom of God advanced, the influence of the demons retreated, for Christ has "disarmed the principalities and powers" by His crucifixion and Resurrection (Col. 2:15). Ephesus would go from a major center of paganism and occult practice to one of evangelization.

It was also during this period that Paul wrote the First Letter to the Corinthians (see 1 Cor 16:8–9). He eventually decided to conclude his missionary journey by visiting the churches of Macedonia and Achaia and then returning to Jerusalem (Acts 19:21). Accordingly, he informed the Corinthians in his letter that he would be coming (1 Cor. 16:5–7). Although Luke does not mention the fact, one of Paul's main objectives in his swing through the Greek mainland was to take up a collection for the church in Jerusalem (1 Cor. 16:1–4). He prepared for the tour by sending ahead Timothy and Erastus, who were "ministering" (*diakonounton*) with him (Acts 19:22) and would help him take up the collection (1 Cor. 16:10). In the meantime, Paul had already begun to plan a fourth missionary journey, which would use Rome as a base to reach the western Mediterranean (see Rom. 15:23–24, 28).

## Gods Made with Hands

As Paul was preparing to leave for Macedonia, a large disturbance arose when the adherents of the goddess Artemis began to agitate against Paul and the disciples (Acts 19:23). Artemis was the Greek goddess of wild animals, and Ephesus was a major center of her cult. Her great temple in Ephesus, the Artemision, attracted worshippers from all over Asia Minor, and generated a great deal of commerce in the process. The disturbance began with a silversmith named Demetrius, "who made silver shrines of Artemis," i.e., smaller replicas of the cult statue in her temple (Acts 19:24). Demetrius gathered the guild of craftsmen and forcefully presented his complaint that Paul's evangelism was threatening both the cult of Artemis and the trade that depended on it. Paul had been teaching, according to Demetrius' pointed but accurate summary, that "gods made with hands are not gods" (Acts 19:26).[2] As Paul progressively evangelized the Ephesians, the "market" for shrines of the goddess began to shrink (Acts 19:27). Thus, Demetrius' concern was simultaneously religious and economic: the business of the craftsmen rested on the worship of Artemis, and "from this business we have our wealth" (Acts 19:25). Demetrius' explicit appeal to wealth did not reflect mere cynicism on his part. Rather, a central purpose of the worship of pagan deities was to obtain earthly benefits. Artemis brought her Ephesian worshippers considerable wealth, and they in turn were genuinely grateful.

### The Enraged Crowd

The craftsmen responded to Demetrius' provocation by rushing into the streets and shouting slogans in honor of Artemis, which soon gathered a crowd. The crowd seized two of Paul's co-workers and took them to the city's large open-air theater, presumably to administer some sort of mob justice (Acts 19:28–29). Upon hearing of the disturbance, Paul sought to go to the theater and address the crowd, but

---

[2] Paul's teaching concerning such idols was drawn from both the prophetic (see Is. 44:9–20; 46:6–7) and wisdom (see Wis. 13:10–19; 15:15–17) traditions.

he was dissuaded from undertaking such a dangerous course of action by the disciples (Acts 19:30). Likewise, the chief officials of Ephesus, called the Asiarchs because of their traditional authority within the province of Asia, prevailed on Paul to stay away (Acts 19:31).

The Jews of Ephesus realized that, as known opponents of idolatry, they too were in great danger from the crowd, and they "put forward" one of their leaders "to make a defense to the people" and so deflect the crowd's anger away from themselves (Acts 19:33). The tactic unfortunately backfired, as the sight of the Jewish leader only inflamed the crowd further. For the next two hours, the enraged pagans would do nothing but shout, "Great is Artemis of the Ephesians!" (Acts 19:34). However, shouting does not make a thing so. With their frenzied cries, the crowd resembled the prophets of Baal who sought to overcome Elijah: "And they . . . called on the name of Baal from morning until noon, saying, 'O Baal, answer us!' But there was no voice, and no one answered" (1 Kings 18:26). At Ephesus as at Mount Carmel, the pagan deity abandoned its adherents and fell silent.

Finally, the town clerk took control of the situation, admonishing the craftsmen to bring any legal charges they might have to the proper administrative officials and the courts (Acts 19:38), just as any political problems should be brought before "the regular assembly" (Acts 19:39). By assembling an unruly mob, the clerk warned, the craftsmen have risked provoking the intervention of the Roman authorities, who would punish rioting severely (Acts 19:40). "And when he had said this, he dismissed the assembly" (Acts 19:41). In the shadow of the *Pax Romana*, the pagan backlash against the Gospel faded as quickly as it had begun.

\* \* \*

## Questions for Discussion

**1.** Read Acts 19:1–6. What is Paul's attitude toward those whose faith is incomplete? What actions can we take to assist those who need further instruction in the faith?

_____

_____

_____

_____

_____

_____

**2.** Read Acts 19:18–20. Paul's missionary strategy consistently involved going into the heart of "enemy territory" with confidence and boldness. How can we pursue an analogous strategy today?

_____

_____

_____

_____

_____

_____

**3.** Read Acts 19:24–27. What are the chief idols and false gods within our culture that act as obstacles to a new evangelization? How can we best overcome them?

_____

_____

_____

_____

_____

_____

## 5

## BREAKING THE BREAD
### —ACTS 20:1–16—

Immediately after the craftsmen's riot, Paul left Ephesus for Macedonia (Acts 20:1; cf. 2 Cor. 2:12–13), as he had been planning to do before his departure was delayed by that disturbance (Acts 19:21–22). The purpose of his swing through Macedonia and Greece was to take up a collection for the church in Jerusalem (2 Cor. 8:1–7). Luke refers to Paul's time in Macedonia very tersely (Acts 20:2), but Paul apparently traveled throughout Macedonia for about a year, gathering up the collection and composing the Second Epistle to the Corinthians. He finally came to Greece, where "he spent three months" completing the collection and composing the Epistle to the Romans (cf. Rom. 15:25–27). He had planned to sail directly for Syria, but upon learning of a plot "against him by the Jews" of the locality, he decided instead to return by the way he had come, through Macedonia and Asia Minor (Acts 20:3).

A number of Paul's co-workers from the various areas that he had evangelized assisted him by transporting the collected funds ahead to Troas in Asia Minor (Acts 20:4–5). Paul, meanwhile, stopped first in Philippi, where he rejoined Luke, who had earlier remained behind in that city (Acts 16:12).[1] "[A]fter the days of Unleavened Bread," which began with Passover and continued throughout the following

---

[1] At this point in the narrative, Luke resumes his use of "we."

week, Paul and Luke sailed together to Troas to meet the larger group (Acts 20:6).

## The Eucharist in Troas

In his description of their sojourn in Troas, Luke gives the only narrative account in Acts of a particular celebration of the Eucharist. He describes this Eucharist, like that on the road to Emmaus (cf. Lk. 24:13, 28, 30), in language that emphasizes the power and presence of the Resurrected Christ. The disciples in Troas gathered "[o]n the first day of the week" (Acts 20:7), a preferred time for the celebration of the Eucharist in commemoration of the Resurrection. When referring to this day, Luke employs an unusual Semitism, writing *te mia ton sabbaton* (literally, "[day] one of the week"), using the cardinal *mia* ("one") rather than the ordinal *prote* ("first"). In so doing, he follows the Septuagint's literal rendering of Genesis 1:5. His manner of expression calls to mind the creation account of Genesis 1 and points to the Eucharist as marking a new creation.[2]

The gathering was planned in order "to break bread," as Luke consistently refers to the Eucharist, suggesting that such liturgies had already become customary on Sundays. During the first part of the liturgy, Paul gave a sermon and "prolonged his speech until midnight" (Acts 20:7), long enough for at least one young man to fall asleep (Acts 20:9). Paul may have spoken for such an unusually long time expecting that he would never visit Troas again.

---

[2] Eugene LaVerdiere, *The Breaking of the Bread: The Development of the Eucharist According to Acts* (Chicago: Liturgy Training Publications, 1998), 94–95.

## Raising the Dead

The liturgy took place in "the upper chamber" on "the third story" of a house (Acts 20:8–9). As Paul spoke, Eutychus, a young man who had been "sitting in the window," fell asleep and slipped out the window to the ground below (Acts 20:9). His fellow disciples rushed down to his aid, only to find him dead. "But Paul went down and bent over him, and embracing him said '. . . his life [*psuche*] is in him,'" upon which Eutychus lived indeed (Acts 20:10). The raising of Eutychus from the dead stands out as the only miracle of this kind that Paul performs in Acts.

The entire episode contains strong echoes of Elijah's visitation of the widow of Zarephath, recounted in 1 Kings 17. During a time of famine, Elijah traveled to the city of Zarephath in the Gentile land of Sidon (1 Kings 17:9). In that city, he was fed by a generous widow "for many days" from her miniscule store of meal and oil, which did not fail due to "the word of the Lord" (1 Kings 17:15–16). The miraculous supply of meal and oil is thus a type of the Eucharist by which the disciple is miraculously fed.

Later, the widow's son became ill and died (1 Kings 17:17–18), whereupon Elijah "carried him up into the upper chamber, . . . stretched himself upon the child" and asked the Lord to "let this child's soul [*psuche*] come into him again" (1 Kings 17:19–21, Greek Old Testament). When the child's life was restored, Elijah told the widow, "See, your son lives" (1 Kings 17:23).

At the beginning of His public ministry, Jesus explicitly cited Elijah's visitation of the widow of

Zarephath as paradigmatic for His own work.[3] After declaring His anointing by the Spirit "to preach good news" (Lk. 4:16–18, 21; cf. Is. 61:1), He told the congregation in the synagogue of Nazareth that "no prophet is acceptable in his own country," for "Elijah was sent . . . only to Zarephath, in the land of Sidon, to a woman who was a widow" (Lk. 4:24, 26). He thereby indicated that the kingdom of God was destined to be inaugurated among not only the Jews but also the Gentiles. Later, He followed Elijah in raising from the dead a "young man" who was "the only son of his mother, . . . a widow" (Lk. 7:12, 14). By these prophetic actions, as with the rest of His words and deeds, Jesus proclaimed and enacted the kingdom of God. Paul's analogous raising of Eutychus in the midst of the Eucharistic liturgy shows that, in the Eucharist, the risen Christ exercises His power to give new life.

## From Passover to Pentecost

When the time for the consecration came, Paul himself broke the bread, highlighting the role of the individual ministerial priesthood (Acts 20:11). Afterwards, Paul "conversed" (*homilesas*) with the congregation. A *homilia* is a company gathered for fellowship.[4] Luke's terminology depicts the Eucharistic congregation as a company united for communion in the new Passover. The next day, the missionaries departed Troas and began traveling southward by ship

---

[3] Michael Duggan, *The Consuming Fire: A Christian Introduction to the Old Testament* (San Francisco: Ignatius Press, 1991), 199.
[4] LaVerdiere, *The Breaking of the Bread,* 212.

down the Aegean coast, crisscrossing between the nearby islands and coastal ports (Acts 20:11, 13–15). Luke's account of their various stops is quite detailed, reflecting his personal knowledge of the journey.

In planning their stops down the coast of Asia Minor, "Paul had decided to sail past Ephesus" (Acts 20:16), the city in which he had evangelized for so long. He may have wished to avoid the danger of persecution in Ephesus, which had already once interfered with his missionary plans. Further trouble now could put at risk the funds he had worked so hard to collect and delay his arrival in Jerusalem, which he wanted to reach by Pentecost.

Pentecost was a major festival on which Jews "from every nation" of the Diaspora traveled to Jerusalem (Acts 2:5). It was on this festival that Christ, following the Ascension, has poured out His Spirit "upon all flesh" (Acts 2:17–18). Paul was eager to deliver to the Jerusalem church the collection he had taken up from the Gentiles as a tangible sign of how widely the Spirit had now been poured out, without regard for nationality or ethnicity (Acts 21:19). This sign was the fruition of the earlier gift of foreign languages (Acts 2:6–12), and he hoped that it would motivate the conversion of the many Jews who would be present for the festival (Acts 2:41).

\*   \*   \*

## Questions for Discussion

**1.** Read 2 Corinthians 8:1–7. Do we generously and enthusiastically give financial support to Catholic apostolates, especially those which directly support evangelization?

_____

_____

_____

_____

**2.** Read Acts 20:7. Paul clearly thought it fitting to expound the Word of God at great length. How seriously do we meditate upon the Word of God given to us in the Scripture readings at Mass?

_____

_____

_____

_____

**3.** Read Acts 20:9–10. In what ways has the power of the Resurrection been manifested in our own lives? Do we understand our active participation in the liturgy and reception of the Eucharist as just such a manifestation?

_____

_____

_____

_____

_____

_____

## 6

## A FINAL FAREWELL
### —ACTS 20:17–21:16—

From Miletus, a city on the coast of Asia Minor about thirty miles south of Ephesus, Paul sent for the elders of the Ephesian church to speak with them one last time (Acts 20:17). Luke earlier described Paul and Barnabas ordaining elders (*presbuteroi*) to lead the local churches they had established (Acts 14:23), and Paul might well have ordained these Ephesian elders himself.[1]

Paul's speech to the Ephesian elders is distinctive in that it is his only speech in Acts given exclusively to members of the Church, as opposed to an audience including the unconverted. The speech is a farewell discourse whose purpose is to instruct those who will succeed Paul as leaders responsible for defending the Sacred Tradition that he had delivered to them.[2] The speech strongly echoes both the language and instruction that Paul gives in his letters.

Paul begins the speech by presenting himself as a model for the disciples to imitate (Acts 20:18; 1 Thess. 2:1–12). He sets forth his own life as an example of a servant of God (Acts 20:19), emphasizing the importance of humility (see Eph. 4:1–2) and the willingness to suffer (see 2 Cor. 2:4; 2 Tim. 1:4). As a true shepherd, Paul did not hesitate to preach whatever was

---

[1] William S. Kurz, SJ, *Farewell Addresses in the New Testament*, ed. Mary Ann Getty, RSM, Zacchaeus Studies: New Testament (Collegeville, MN: Michael Glazier, The Liturgical Press, 1990), 36. Paul later gave instructions for the treatment of elders in Ephesus (1 Tim. 5:17–19).
[2] Ibid., 50.

spiritually profitable, even when it was unpleasant (Acts 20:20). His testimony "to both Jews and to Greeks" centered on "repentance to God and of faith in our Lord Jesus Christ" (Acts 20:21). Repentance (*metanoia*) is not a feeling or vague attitude but a complete change of heart and mind that entails the renunciation of concrete sins, which Paul does not hesitate elsewhere to enumerate (see Gal. 5:19–21).[3] Likewise, faith is directed to the person of Jesus Christ, whose redemptive work is proclaimed in the Gospel so as to make faith possible (Rom. 10:14).

## Guardians of the Flock

Paul informs the elders that he is leaving for Jerusalem, convicted by the Holy Spirit of the necessity to make the journey, but ignorant of its outcome except that "imprisonment and afflictions await me" (Acts 20:22–23). Paul viewed his own sufferings not as reversals contrary to the plan of God, but as a glorious offering that should confirm the faith of the disciples (Eph. 3:13).[4] He has no fear for his life, for his suffering will only fulfill his calling on the road to Damascus, when Christ declared him "a chosen instrument of mine to carry my name before the Gentiles and kings and the sons of Israel; for I will show him how much he must suffer for the sake of my name" (Acts 9:15–16). Christ has set before Paul a "course" he must run (2 Tim. 4:7) consisting of the "ministry . . . to testify to the gospel." Paul therefore devotes himself

---

[3] Ibid., 38.
[4] Jesus similarly interpreted His impending suffering during His farewell address to the apostles (Jn. 13:18–19).

to proclaiming the life, death, and Resurrection of Jesus, by which He has become King of the kingdom that Paul now preaches.[5] The "grace of God" has thus been poured forth through particular historical events that have transformed the world (Acts 20:24).

Paul tells the elders that they "will see my face no more" (Acts 20:25) and solemnly proclaims himself "innocent of the blood of all of you, for I did not shrink from declaring to you the whole counsel of God" (Acts 20:26-27). As in his similar declaration in the synagogue of Corinth (Acts 18:6), Paul is referring to the prophetic responsibility to deliver completely the Word of God (cf. Ezek. 3:16-21). He admonishes the elders to care for "the flock," employing a familiar prophetic metaphor for the People of God (cf. Mic. 5:4; Is. 40:11; Jer. 13:17; Ezek. 34:12). The elders have been made "guardians" or overseers (episkopoi) of that flock, responsible for guarding the Church especially against false doctrine (cf. 1 Tim. 4:16).[6] The elders' zealous oversight should flow directly from their knowledge that the Body of Christ was "obtained with his own blood" and so redeemed by His sacrificial death (Acts 20:28; cf. Titus 2:13-14). Continuing the prophetic metaphor, Paul warns that "after my departure fierce wolves will come in among you, not sparing the flock" (Acts 20:29; cf. Ezek. 22:27). The fierce wolves are not external enemies, but members of the Church who teach false doctrine, "speaking perverse things, to draw away the disciples" (Acts 20:30).

---

[5] Wright, *What Saint Paul Really Said*, 45.
[6] Kurz, *Farewell Addresses in the New Testament*, 46.

## Building the House

Therefore, the elders must "be alert" and attend to the Word of God, "which is able to build you up" (Acts 20:31–32). The term "to build up" (*oikodomeo*) literally means "to build a house" and depicts the Church as the house of God. Paul teaches that the gifts of grace are given for the sake of apostolate, in order to build up the household of faith (Eph. 4:11–13). If the elders cooperate with this grace, they too will receive "the inheritance among all those who are sanctified," those who through Baptism have been adopted into the household (*oikos*) as sons (Acts 20:32; cf. Eph. 1:18; Col. 1:12).

Paul had consistently and deliberately supported his apostolate by his own manual labor (Acts 20:33–34; 2 Thess. 3:7–8). This way of life allowed him better to reach the poor outside the Church and corresponds to the teaching of Christ: "It is more blessed to give than to receive" (Acts 20:35).[7] For Paul, this principle is not so much a generic injunction to generosity as a motivation for productive labor. Through such labor, the disciple of Christ endeavors to make himself available for apostolate, becoming a benefactor to others rather than dependent on another's aid. He may thereby attain a way of life encompassing the unity of nature and grace from which apostolate flows. Regarding the convert from even the most disadvantaged of backgrounds, Paul instructs, "let him labor, doing honest work with his hands, so that he may be able to give to those in need" (Eph. 4:28; cf. 2 Thess. 3:10).

---

[7] These words of Christ are recorded only here in Acts on the lips of Paul.

## Sailing for Jerusalem

After the discourse, the elders prayed with Paul, grieving "that they should see his face no more," and accompanied him to the ship (Acts 20:36–38). Paul and the missionary party, including Luke, departed and continued on ship from port to port, eventually arriving at Tyre in Phoenicia (Acts 21:1–3). There was a community of disciples in Phoenicia, which had been evangelized shortly after the martyrdom of Stephen (Acts 11:19) and which Paul had visited on an earlier trip to Jerusalem (Acts 15:3). During the missionaries' stay in Tyre, the Phoenician disciples attempted to persuade Paul "not to go on to Jerusalem" (Acts 21:4), just as Peter had attempted to dissuade Jesus from His final journey to Jerusalem (Mt. 16:21–22). From this point to the end of Acts, Paul's experiences will echo those of Jesus' final journey.[8] Without disputing either the spiritual motives or the prudence of the Phoenician disciples, Paul calmly persevered in his plans, having already accepted the possibility of martyrdom. The missionaries remained in Tyre for a week, after which the disciples prayed with them and accompanied them back to their ship (Acts 21:5–6).

From Tyre, they sailed down to Caesarea, the last port on the route to Jerusalem (Acts 21:7–8). There they stayed with Philip, who, as one of the original seven deacons (Acts 7:5–6), had evangelized the coast of Judea up to Caesarea (cf. Acts 8:40). Luke notes that Philip's four daughters were virgins (*parthenoi*), possibly consecrated as such

---

[8] Kurz, *Farewell Addresses in the New Testament*, 35.

(see 1 Cor. 7:25-40), and had received the gift of prophecy (Acts 21:9).[9]

After a few days, the prophet Agabus, who had long before predicted the famine of AD 44-46 in Judea (Acts 11:28), arrived in Caesarea (Acts 21:10). Upon meeting the missionaries among the disciples, Agabus "took Paul's girdle and bound his own feet and hands," performing a symbolic act in the manner of the Hebrew prophets (see Is. 20:2-4; Jer. 19:10-11; 27:2, 12; Ezek. 4:1-3). He then interpreted the symbolic action for all assembled with a formal prophetic oracle: "Thus says the Holy Spirit, 'So shall the Jews at Jerusalem bind the man who owns this girdle'" (Acts 21:11). Agabus further declared that these Jews shall "deliver him [Paul] into the hands of the Gentiles," echoing Jesus' predictions of His own Passion (cf. Lk. 9:44; 18:32).

Paul had already known in a general way that he could anticipate "imprisonment and afflictions" (Acts 20:23). Agabus has now removed all doubt that such a fate awaited him shortly in Jerusalem. Paul is thereby led to the final moment of trial and commitment, like Jesus in the Garden of Gethsemane (cf. Mk. 14:32-41). Upon hearing Agabus' prophecy, both Paul's fellow missionaries and the other disciples "begged him not to go up to Jerusalem" (Acts 21:12). Paul, however, remonstrated with them for their inconstancy, declaring his willingness to accept a death like that of Jesus, witnessing to the Jews of Jerusalem (Acts 21:13).

---

[9] In the centuries to follow, many great and holy women, such as Saint Hildegaard of Bingen, Saint Catherine of Siena, and Saint Teresa of Avila were to receive the gift of prophecy.

\* \* \*

## Questions for Discussion

**1.** Read Acts 20:20, 27, 29. Why does Paul emphasize that, in his own preaching, he "did not shrink from declaring" the faith in its entirety? How does the example he set for the elders relate to his subsequent warning about the "fierce wolves" who will attack "the flock"?

_____

_____

_____

_____

**2.** Read Acts 20:33–35. How does Paul base the possibility of serving others in a prior commitment to productive labor? What insight does this give us into the nature of charity?

_____

_____

_____

_____

_____

**3.** Read Acts 20:24; 21:4–5, 12–13. As his third missionary journey draws to a close, in what ways does Paul see his ministry nearing its completion?

_____

_____

_____

_____

## 7

## STORM AT JERUSALEM
### —ACTS 20:17–23:22—

Traveling with Luke and the missionary co-workers who had joined him earlier (Acts 20:4), Paul finally arrived in Jerusalem (Acts 21:17). The next day, the missionary party visited James, who served as the head of the Jerusalem church after the departure of the apostles, and the assembled elders of that church (Acts 21:18). Paul described the many "things that God had done among the Gentiles through his ministry" (Acts 21:19) and presumably delivered the collection from his missionary churches. James and the elders "glorified God" for the success of Paul's missionary work but quickly turned to a more local concern. "[M]any thousands" of the Jews of Jerusalem had become disciples of Christ, and "they are all zealous for the law" (Acts 21:20). Such widespread zeal for the Deuteronomic Law testified to the continuing influence of the Pharisee party within the Jerusalem church (cf. Acts 15:5). The concern was that a rumor had been circulated that Paul formally instructed (*katechethesan*) the Jews in the Diaspora to apostatize (*apostasian*) from the Deuteronomic Law, "telling them not to circumcise their children or observe the customs" (Acts 21:21). James and the elders did not endorse the rumor but were nevertheless concerned that the Jewish disciples "have been told" such things, presumably by opponents of the Church.

## From Covenant to Covenant

Paul did not, in fact, teach or hold such a position. He had no objection to Jewish disciples continuing to observe the Deuteronomic Law and did so himself whenever necessary to avoid scandal (cf. Acts 16:3). The apostles had not previously set forth any definitive teaching concerning the proper behavior of Jewish disciples toward the Deuteronomic Law. Their previous decisions concerning the Law had addressed only *Gentile* disciples. They had first decided that Gentile disciples need not be circumcised and follow the Law *prior* to Baptism (Acts 11:18). They had then decided that Gentile disciples need not be circumcised and follow the Law *after* Baptism (Acts 15:5–10). However, the obligations of *Jewish* disciples in this regard had not been expressly addressed.

Subsequent teaching of the Church did clarify the overall status of the Deuteronomic Law.[1] During the forty-year period from AD 30 to 70, Jewish disciples were permitted to continue observing the Law, as long as they did not hold such observance to be necessary for salvation. The latter qualification follows from Peter's declaration that the Jewish disciples "shall be saved through the grace of the Lord Jesus, just as they [the Gentile disciples] will" (Acts 15:11), making the grace of Christ the only criterion of salvation for Jews and Gentiles alike. The People of God was undergoing a transition of covenants and therefore of covenantal laws, from the Deuteronomic Law to the New Law.

---

[1] The chief source is *Cantate Domino*, Council of Florence (1442). See Pimentel, *Witnesses of the Messiah*, 131 for further references and discussion.

During this period of transition, the force of the Deuteronomic Law had not completely fallen away, as it would after the judgment of Jerusalem and the destruction of the temple, when the transition of covenants would be complete.[2]

## The Vow of Piety

James and the elders feared that the rumor might cause scandal, damaging the evangelistic witness of the Jerusalem church to the Jews of the city (cf. Acts 21:22). To mitigate the danger of scandal, they proposed that Paul assist four disciples with the completion of their Nazarite vow (see Num. 6:1–21). The four men had apparently contracted some form of ritual uncleanness while under the vow and thus fallen under the additional requirement of a seven-day ritual purification (cf. Num. 6:9), followed by sacrifices on eighth day (cf. Num. 6:10–12).[3] Although he was not himself under a Nazarite vow, Paul was urged to join the men for their purification (perhaps because of his sojourn among the Gentiles) and assume the expenses for the subsequent temple sacrifices (Acts 21:23–24). The payment of such expenses was considered to be an act of great piety. Because the devotional act would be visible to the entire community, James and the elders hoped that it would counter the false accusations against Paul and therefore allow the Jerusalem church to fully embrace Paul's mission among the Gentiles without fear of scandal. James

[2] See Pimentel, *Witnesses of the Messiah,* 139–140.
[3] Num. 6:9 refers expressly to corpse uncleanness but was interpreted in latter rabbinical teaching to cover more general cases of ritual uncleanness.

hastened to acknowledge that Gentile disciples were not required to observe the Deuteronomic Law but only to follow the prior decree of the Council of Jerusalem (cf. Acts 21:25; Acts 15:20, 28–29).[4]

The next day, Paul took part in the purification rite with the four men, accompanied them to the temple, and gave notice to initiate the seven-day period and thereby fix the date on which the sacrifices for completion would take place (Acts 21:26). On each of the subsequent days of the purification period, Paul and the four men came to the temple, and all seemed to be progressing smoothly. However, "when the seven days were almost completed," Paul was accosted in the temple by Jews from Asia Minor, who probably knew of him from his extended stay in Ephesus (cf. Acts 19:8–10). It was common for Jews from the Diaspora to be in Jerusalem during the Pentecost festival. The Jews from Asia Minor "stirred up all the crowd," accusing Paul of "teaching men everywhere against the people and the law and this place" (Acts 21:27–28). In the first of many echoes of Stephen's trial and martyrdom, the accusation made against Paul closely parallels that made against Stephen (cf. Acts 6:12–13). Because he had been seen with a Gentile co-worker in the city, Paul was also falsely accused of having defiled the temple by bringing Gentiles into the inner court or "holy place" reserved for Jews, which would have been a capital offense (Acts 21:28–29).

---

[4] See Pimentel, *Witnesses of the Messiah,* 136–139 for an explanation of the decree.

## The Hand of Rome

A large crowd "seized Paul and dragged him out" of the inner court, intending to beat him to death, when the Roman tribune and soldiers intervened (Acts 21:30–32). The tribune was the military commander of the cohort, which consisted of between 600 and 1000 soldiers. The Jerusalem cohort was stationed in the great fortress Antonia, adjacent to and overlooking the temple, with quick access by stairway to the court of the Gentiles. The tribune arrested Paul "and ordered him to be bound with two chains," thus fulfilling the prophecy of Agabus (Acts 21:33; cf. Acts 21:11). Paul will remain a prisoner of the Roman authorities for the remainder of Acts.

The tribune attempted to find out what was going on, but was unable due to the unruliness of the crowd. Therefore, he ordered Paul to be taken into the fortress Antonia for further examination (Acts 21:34). At the top of the steps, Paul addressed the tribune in Greek. In response, the tribune voiced his suspicion that Paul was one of the recent insurrectionists, who were prone to initiate violent disturbances in the temple area during the festival periods (cf. Acts 21:37–38). Paul protested that he was no insurrectionist but "a Jew, from Tarsus in Cilicia, a citizen of no mean city," and asked the tribune for permission to address the crowd (Acts 21:39). Wanting to know more about the man at the center of the tumult, the tribune complied.

## The Apologia for His Life

Paul did not naively imagine that his words would be favorably received by the crowd. He had known

his life would be in danger when he entered
Jerusalem (Acts 20:22–23; 21:13; cf. Rom. 15:31). He
knew well the disposition of the Hellenist Jews in
Jerusalem toward those who pursued the mission to
the Gentiles. He remembered the day he had held the
garments of those who stoned Stephen outside the
walls of the city (Acts 7:58). He remembered the
ferocity with which he himself had persecuted the
disciples of Christ to the death. He remembered the
attempts to murder him when, after his vision of
Christ, he returned to Jerusalem to preach in the
Hellenist synagogues (Acts 9:28–29). He remembered the many beatings and attempts on his life by
Jews in the Diaspora. In spite of all this, he shared
James' determination to reach as many Jews in
Jerusalem as possible (cf. Rom. 10:1–2), for there are
always some who hear and believe.

Standing at the top of the steps, Paul began to
speak to the crowd "in the Hebrew language," probably meaning Aramaic, the common language of
Jews in Palestine (Acts 21:40). By shifting from Greek
to Aramaic, Paul was not so much appealing to Jews
as opposed to Gentiles, but to the "Hebrews" or
Aramaic-speaking Jews as opposed to the "Hellenists"
or Greek-speaking Jews. It was these Hellenists who
had led the opposition to Stephen (Acts 6:1, 9–11).[5]
Paul addressed the people as "[b]rethren and fathers,"
the same form of address with which Stephen had
begun his own speech (Acts 22:1; cf. Acts 7:2).
"[F]athers" may refer to members of the Sanhedrin

---

[5] Pimentel, *Witnesses of the Messiah,* 69, 71.

present in the audience. Paul refers to his impending speech as a legal-style defense (*apologia*). The speech is the first of the many defenses that Paul will deliver while under Roman custody.

The speech as a whole is a flashback, narrating Paul's life from his youth until the beginning of his participation in the Gentile mission. In the speech, Paul highlights his Jewish identity, illustrating through his personal testimony the movement of the Gospel from Israel to the nations. Though born in Tarsus, he was "brought up in this city" and "educated according to the strict manner of the law of our fathers" (Acts 22:3). Paul's youthful education in Jerusalem had not previously been mentioned in Acts. He was "zealous for God as you all are this day," and, in this zeal, he "persecuted this Way to the death" (Acts 22:3–4). Paul's history of persecuting the Church may have been known to many in Jerusalem, particularly in light of its formal authorization by the Sanhedrin (Acts 22:5).

Paul then recounts his vision of Christ on the road to Damascus and the loss of his sight (Acts 22:6–11),[6] which is restored in Damascus by Ananias, "a devout man according to the law, well spoken of by all the Jews who lived there" (Acts 22:12–13). Ananias' reputation for devout observance of the Deuteronomic Law undergirds Paul's contention that the mission to the Gentiles is the fulfillment of God's promise to bring the nations into covenantal relation with Himself. Ananias declared that "[t]he God of our

---

[6] Paul's first-person account complements the earlier narrative account in Acts 9:1–19.

fathers" had appointed Paul "to see the Just One" and then serve as "a witness for him to all men" (Acts 22:14–15). Ananias thereby confirmed that the mission to the Gentiles, far from being of pagan inspiration, was directly commanded by the God of Abraham, Isaac, and Jacob (cf. Acts 3:13). This mission centers on "the Just One," as both Peter and Stephen had described the Messiah (cf. Acts 3:14–15; 7:52).

### The Memory of Stephen

After his baptism in Damascus, Paul returned to Jerusalem (Act 9:26). While "praying in the temple" (Acts 22:17), he had a second vision in which he was commissioned, like the prophet Isaiah, to serve as a messenger of God in spite of the resistance he was certain to encounter in Jerusalem (cf. Is. 6:1–10).[7] Jesus instructed Paul to "get quickly out of Jerusalem, because they will not accept your testimony about me" (Acts 22:18), a warning applicable not only to Paul's rejection when first forced by the Hellenists to flee Jerusalem (Acts 9:28–30), but also to his situation now, when he will be rejected again. Paul was disconcerted by this command, believing that he ought to be the most credible of witnesses. He exclaimed that, as his enemies well know, he himself had fiercely persecuted the disciples of Jesus (Acts 22:19). As the most important example of such persecution, he invoked his role in the martyrdom of Stephen (Acts 22:20).

---

[7] Acts mentions this second vision only in this speech.

The memory of Stephen is central to the meaning of Paul's speech, for Paul saw his own vocation as that of the successor of Stephen. In an act of supreme divine irony, Paul was given Stephen's mission, with its distinctive vision of the universality of the Church, after Stephen's death. Stephen had preached that the failure of many in Israel to accept the Word of God was rooted in their idolatrous attachment to the visible markers of the Deuteronomic covenant, such as the Promised Land, the Law, and the temple.[8] This critique of the corruption of Israel's faith led to Stephen's death at the hands of the angry crowd. Stephen's mission, however, was to be carried on by Paul, and so Jesus repeated that Paul must leave Jerusalem. Like Isaiah (see Is. 6:8), Paul was sent forth from the temple, only now the prophetic destination is "far away to the Gentiles" (Acts 22:21).

Paul's description of being commanded by the Messiah to commence the mission to the nations enraged the crowd (Acts 22:22). Such a mission implies that the covenantal promises given to Abraham and the prophets are being fulfilled by the inclusion of the nations, contradicting the prevailing theologies centered on ethnicity. If the God of Israel is now bringing the Gentiles into covenantal relation with Himself, bringing them into the new temple built up by the Messiah, then it is the opponents of the Gentile mission, rather than Paul, who are apostates. Israel's calling was to serve as "a light to the

---

[8] Pimentel, *Witnesses of the Messiah,* 73.

nations" (Is. 49:6), not as a bulwark of ethnic privilege.[9] Less than a decade before the city and temple would be destroyed, Paul has again placed before the Jews of Jerusalem the call to repentance, and again many rejected the call.

## Before the Sanhedrin

Both the theological import of Paul's words and the crowd's frenzied response were opaque to the tribune. Determined to discover the cause of the threatening disorder, he ordered Paul to be taken into the fortress Antonia and interrogated by scourging (Acts 22:23–24). Paul, however, did not consider it an apt moment to receive a Roman scourging, and so, more swiftly than he had at Philippi, he invoked his rights as a Roman citizen (cf. Acts 16:37). As soon as "they had tied him up with the thongs," Paul archly asked the attending centurion if it was "lawful for you to scourge a man who is a Roman citizen, and uncondemned?" (Acts 22:25). When Paul's Roman citizenship was reported to the tribune, all attempts to forcibly interrogate him ceased, as such interrogation of Roman citizens by military officers was a serious crime under Roman law (cf. Acts 22:26–29).

Nevertheless, the tribune still wished to know the cause of the agitation against Paul. He therefore exercised his authority to convene the Sanhedrin and brought Paul to appear before it (Acts 22:30). Speaking to the Sanhedrin, Paul did not describe his attitude toward the Deuteronomic Law, but simply declared that he had "lived before God in all good

---

[9] Ibid., 76.

conscience up to this day" (Acts 23:1). Ananias, the high priest, took Paul's words to be insolent and ordered the attendants "to strike him on the mouth" (Acts 23:2). Paul swiftly countered that the high priest's command violated the very Law he pretended to uphold[10] and declared, "God shall strike you" (Acts 23:3). Paul's exclamation was no mere spontaneous expression of anger but rather a specific biblical reference. The phrase "[t]he Lord will smite you" is found four times in Scripture, all in the portion of Deuteronomy 28 that records the curses of the Deuteronomic covenant (Deut. 28:22, 27, 28, 35). These curses describe the various forms of death that the Israelites would suffer under attack by Gentile armies if they violated the covenant. Paul's words indicated that the high priest would in some way be caught up in the Deuteronomic curses. As it turned out, Ananias would be murdered at the beginning of the revolt against Rome by the Jewish insurrectionists themselves.[11]

Yet Paul wished not to quarrel with the high priest but to testify to the Gospel. Accordingly, when he "perceived that one part" of the Sanhedrin "were Sadducees and the other Pharisees," he seized the opportunity to broach a teaching related to the Gospel, declaring that, as a Pharisee himself, he was on trial "with respect to the hope and the resurrection of the dead" (Acts 23:6). By affirming the resurrection of the dead, Paul engendered a sharp dissension between the two factions on the Sanhedrin, while

---

[10] Stephen had criticized the Sanhedrin on similar grounds (cf. Acts 7:53).
[11] Josephus, *The Wars of the Jews*, II.17.9.

seeming to align himself with one (cf. Acts 23:7–8). He thereby demonstrated to the tribune that the fierce hostility to him stemmed from theological teachings that were of no proper concern to the Roman authorities. At the same time, he subtly alluded to (without explicitly raising) the truly fundamental issue: the Resurrection of Jesus.

The Pharisees were willing to concede that Paul's visions may have been of "a spirit or an angel" (Acts 23:9). The Sadducees, in contrast, could not acknowledge even this limited possibility because they denied the existence of such. In any case, neither group conceded that Jesus of Nazareth might have appeared to Paul. By their refusal to accept the Resurrection of Jesus, the Jerusalem leaders, including the Pharisees among them, rejected the saving work of the God of Israel.

When the quarreling in the Sanhedrin grew violent, the tribune was forced to have Paul retrieved by soldiers and returned to the fortress Antonia (Acts 23:10). However, Paul's opponents were not satisfied to have him remain in Roman custody. In collusion with the Sanhedrin, they entered into a plot to murder him (Acts 23:12–14). The Sanhedrin was to request that Paul be returned for further questioning, and, as he approached, Paul's opponents would ambush and kill him (Acts 23:15). Through the intervention of Paul's nephew, the tribune learned of the plot and ordered that Paul be taken under guard to Caesarea (Acts 23:16–22).

\*    \*    \*

## Questions for Discussion

**1.** Read Acts 21:20–22; Luke 17:1–2; the *Catechism*, nos. 2284–85, 2475–77. Paul has been accused of teaching a doctrine that he neither taught nor held. When does one have a duty to vindicate the truth concerning one's reputation? What are the chief evils that flow from scandal? What are the responsibilities of leaders in regard to the danger of scandal?

_____

_____

_____

_____

_____

_____

**2.** Read Acts 21:23–24, 26; Mt. 6:5–6. What are Paul's intentions in participating in the purification rite and paying the men's expenses? With what intentions should one perform publicly visible acts of piety? Should one ever perform an act of piety merely to be seen by others?

_____

_____

_____

_____

_____

_____

**3.** Read Acts 21:27–30. Are Paul's opponents more interested in faithfulness to God or in ethnic identity? How can a worldly concern for ethnic identity distort our commitment to revealed truth?

_____

_____

_____

_____

_____

_____

## 8

## On Trial
### —Acts 23:23–26:32—

Having received word of the plot against Paul's life, the tribune quickly grasped the scope of the threat and concluded that Paul was no longer safe in Jerusalem. Because he was obliged to ensure due process for a Roman citizen in his charge, he took action to protect Paul, ordering an escort of several hundred soldiers to transport Paul to Caesarea, the Roman capital of Judea, sixty miles northwest of Jerusalem (Acts 23:23). Paul was to be delivered to Felix, governor of Judea from AD 52 to 60 (Acts 23:24). The tribune also sent a letter to Felix in which he acknowledged that, as far as he had been able to ascertain, Paul has not been charged with anything "deserving death" or even "imprisonment" (Acts 23:25–29). Rather, his chief reason for sending Paul to Caesarea was for Paul's own protection (cf. Acts 23:30). Accordingly, the soldiers took Paul and delivered him to Felix, who ordered that he be kept under guard in "Herod's praetorium," a palace of Herod the Great's that had served as the residence of the Roman governor from the time that Judea became a Roman province (Acts 23:31–35).

In Caesarea, Paul's accusers continued to press their charges, only now they were forced to present their case in a Roman court, which they could not control. The high priest Ananias soon arrived with members of the Sanhedrin and a lawyer named Tertullus, who delivered the charges against Paul before Felix (Acts 24:1–9). Paul was thereby for the

first time given the opportunity to address the highest
Roman authority in Palestine (Acts 24:10–21). In his
defense before Felix, Paul emphasized his adherence
to the Hebrew prophets and his consequent hope in
the resurrection of the dead (Acts 24:14–15; cf. Dan.
12:2). He explained that the motive for his travel to
Jerusalem was strictly to deliver the alms he had collected for the Jerusalem church (cf. Acts 24:17) and
demanded that the "Jews from Asia," the supposed
witnesses to his alleged offenses, appear before Felix
to bring their charges, as required by Roman law (Acts
24:18–19).

However, Felix was less interested in the merits of
Paul's case than in the possibilities it afforded for
extracting some personal or political advantage.
Accordingly, he delayed passing judgment on the
case and returned Paul to custody. Although he
promised to decide the case when he received further information from the tribune, he never did so
(Acts 24:22). Felix kept Paul imprisoned, but with
liberty to meet freely with his co-workers (Acts
24:23). Thus began an extended period of imprisonment, later continued at Rome, during which Paul
wrote his so-called "captivity epistles."[1] Felix inter-
mittently summoned Paul to discuss the Christian
faith, but with little apparent effect on his own
beliefs or attitude toward Paul (Acts 24:24–25), and,
after two years, he was replaced as governor by
Festus (Acts 24:27).

---

[1] Epistles probably written during this period include Colossians,
Ephesians, Philemon, and Philippians.

## Appeal to Rome

When Festus arrived in Palestine, he visited Jerusalem to meet the chief priests and other Jewish leaders, who requested that Paul be returned to Jerusalem for trial. However, far from desiring a trial, they were secretly "planning an ambush to kill him on the way" (Acts 25:1–3). Festus instructed the leaders instead to come to Caesarea with him and there present their charges against Paul (Acts 25:4–5). The Jewish leaders complied, but their charges were no more persuasive than they had been previously (Acts 25:6–7). Paul again denied breaking either Roman law or the "law of the Jews," which the Romans allowed to remain partially in force in Judea (Acts 25:8). Festus, unaware of the murder plot and "wishing to do the Jews a favor," proposed that the trial be held in Jerusalem (Acts 25:9).

Paul correctly surmised that his life would be in great danger were he transferred back to Jerusalem. He was perfectly willing to face any charge of a capital offense according to Roman law, knowing himself to be innocent and able to mount an effective defense. However, in order to ensure that his case would be heard before a Roman rather than Judean court, he exercised his right as a Roman citizen to have his case transferred to the imperial court in Rome, and Festus granted his request (Acts 25:10–12).

While Festus was preparing Paul's transfer to Rome, King Agrippa II, who had been given rule over various territories in northern Palestine by the Emperor Claudius, made a courtesy visit to the new governor in accordance with expected protocol (Acts 25:13). Festus privately described Paul's case to

Agrippa, acknowledging that Paul had committed no offense against Roman law (Acts 25:14–18). With detached indifference to its import, he reported that the central point of contention between Paul and his opponents was the former's assertion that Jesus was alive (cf. Acts 25:19). Agrippa requested to hear Paul himself, and Festus complied, giving Paul the opportunity for a more thorough hearing before the highest authorities in Palestine (Acts 25:22–23).

### Before King and Governor

Paul's appearance before Agrippa is the longest and most important of the legal defenses that Paul offers in Acts.[2] Before the appearance begins, Paul has already been effectively absolved by Festus of the charge of sedition (Acts 25:25). The ostensible purpose of the appearance is merely to allow Agrippa to assist Festus in the preparation of a report to accompany Paul's appeal to the imperial court in Rome. Paul is therefore able to address freely the theological concerns that have caused the Jerusalem leadership to bring charges against him.

Paul's argument in the speech is prophetic in both content and mode. In content, the argument is centered on a recurring appeal to the Hebrew prophets. In mode, the speech arranges autobiographical information so as to highlight Paul's commission as a prophet of the New Covenant.[3] In both aspects, the speech is aimed at persuasively presenting the

---

[2] Rosenblatt, *Paul the Accused*, 81.
[3] This prophetic emphasis largely accounts for the inclusion of different details in the account of Paul's vision on the road to Damascus as compared with the accounts in Acts 9 and 22.

Gospel to Agrippa, a man reputed to be committed to Judaism as well as a favored client of Rome.

Paul's appearance before Agrippa is prophetic in yet another way. It is a fulfillment of Jesus' prophecy in the Olivet discourse that, prior to the destruction of Jerusalem and the temple, the disciples would be arrested and "brought before kings and governors for my name's sake," giving them an opportunity to "bear testimony" (Lk. 21:12–13).[4] Jesus applied this prophecy to Paul in particular in His revelation to Ananias (cf. Acts 9:15).

### The Hope of Our Twelve Tribes

Paul begins his address to Agrippa by recognizing the king as one who is expert in the various strands of Judaism. He then launches into his autobiographical account of how he came to be in his present position (Acts 26:2–3). He emphasizes his long identification with the Pharisees, who strongly upheld the authority of the Hebrew prophets (Acts 26:4–5), thereby preparing the way for his argument that the Gospel is in continuity with the teaching of those prophets.

Paul next sets forth the thematic statement of his speech, that he is "on trial for hope in the promise made by God to our fathers, to which our twelve tribes hope to attain" (Acts 26:6–7). The "promise made by God" is the promise of covenantal restoration for Israel given by God to the prophets, the fulfillment of which has begun with the Resurrection of the Messiah. The key to Paul's interpretation of this promise lies in his reference to the "twelve tribes."

---

4 Rosenblatt, *Paul the Accused*, 82.

## All Israel Restored

The twelve tribes of Israel had been united under the monarchy of David and his son Solomon. However, after the death of Solomon, the ten northern tribes broke away from the Davidic monarchy and formed the independent kingdom of Israel. These ten northern tribes were eventually conquered by the Assyrians and dispersed among the nations of the Near East. Only the two southern tribes of Judah and Benjamin remained in the rump kingdom of Judah. Nevertheless, Paul is keenly aware that the key prophetic texts concerning the covenantal restoration of Israel expressly pertain to *all* of Israel, the ten northern tribes as well as the two southern tribes. For example, Jeremiah's prophecy of the New Covenant (Jer. 31:1, 9–10, 31) and Ezekiel's prophecy of the gathering of Israelites from the nations (Ezek. 36:22–25; 37:16–19) both include the northern tribes.

The problem for Jews of the first century was to understand how the restoration of all twelve tribes could occur when ten of them had been thoroughly absorbed by the nations. Paul's bold answer is the "good news" that the Messiah is now sending His Spirit to Israelites and Gentiles alike among those very nations, bringing all who place their faith in Him to new life in a restored Israel. The Gospel is therefore the true hope for the restoration of all Israel, however much it has come to be opposed by some Jews (cf. Rom. 11:26). Ironically, it is for "this hope" that Paul is now "accused by Jews" (Acts 26:7), suggesting that his opponents have abandoned belief in the restoration of the twelve tribes and constricted their hope to the southern tribes of Judah and Benjamin. They have come to think of the restoration of Israel in natural terms, constrained by the natural possibilities attainable by natural means. In contrast, God has planned a far greater restoration through the supernatural kingdom inaugurated by the Resurrection of the Messiah. Because the resurrection of the dead is a central Pharisaic belief, it should not be deemed incredible that the Resurrection of the Messiah has come to pass (Acts 26:8), and if it has, then the supernatural restoration has begun.

### The Servant of the Lord

Paul describes his persecution of the Church and reveals, for the first time in Acts, that he was directly involved in the deaths of disciples other than Stephen (Acts 26:9–11). He then recounts in vivid detail his vision of Jesus on the road to Damascus, seeking through his description to convince Agrippa that the vision was no hallucination (Acts 26:12–13). In this telling of the event, Paul relates that Jesus admonished him that "It is hard [skleron] for you to kick against the goads" (Acts 26:14). The notion of "hardness" echoes the biblical idiom for resistance to grace, while "to kick against the goads" refers to resistance in a strenuous but futile manner.

Paul was commanded to "stand upon your feet," recalling the prophetic commissioning of Ezekiel (see Ezek. 2:1), so that he could serve as a "witness" to Jesus like Stephen before him (Acts 26:16). Jesus declared that He would send Paul to both "the people" of Israel and the Gentiles "to open their eyes, that they may turn from darkness to light and from the power of Satan to God" (Acts 26:17–18). By proclaiming the

Gospel, Paul would serve as an instrument of the Servant of the Lord, who was given "as a covenant to the people, a light to the nations, to open the eyes that are blind, to bring out the prisoners from the dungeon, from the prison those who sit in darkness" (Is. 42:6–7). Not only does salvation spiritually enlighten the individual disciple, but evangelization advances the kingdom of God over and against the kingdom of this world under the authority of Satan. Those who enter the kingdom of God therefore receive "release" (*aphesis*) from the prison of sin "and a place among those who are sanctified by faith" (Acts 26:18).

## The Christ Must Suffer

Paul describes his subsequent obedience to "the heavenly vision," resulting in his evangelism "at Jerusalem and throughout all the country of Judea, and also to the Gentiles" (Acts 26:19–20), tracing out the programmatic itinerary given to the apostles by Jesus before His Ascension (cf. Acts 1:8). It was the inclusion of the Gentiles in Paul's mission that inflamed his Jewish opponents and motivated them to seize him in the temple (cf. Acts 26:21).

God has given Paul the grace to proclaim the Gospel as the fulfillment of the teaching of the prophets, "that the Christ must suffer, and that, by being the first to rise from the dead, he would proclaim light both to the people and to the Gentiles" (Acts 26:22–23; cf. 1 Cor. 15:20–23). Psalm 89 described the suffering of the Messiah and established the basis for identifying the Messiah and the Servant of the Lord (Ps. 89:38–39, 49–51). Isaiah, in turn, taught that the Servant of the Lord would greatly suffer (Is. 49:4; 53:3) but would somehow be restored by God (Is. 49:7–8; 53:10–11) so as in turn "to raise up the tribes of Jacob and to restore the preserved of Israel," acting "as a light to the nations, that my salvation may reach to the end of the earth" (Is. 49:6). The death and Resurrection of the Messiah inaugurates the fulfillment of this covenantal restoration.

Festus found Paul's argument to be incomprehensible, based as it was on Hebrew prophecy, and accused him of madness (cf. Acts 26:24). Paul protested that, on the contrary, his words were temperate (*sophrosune*), reflecting passions and lower faculties under the control of reason (cf. Acts 26:25). He spoke freely (*parresiazomai*) of the Gospel because of his trust in Agrippa's knowledge of the salient prophetic background. Moreover, those claims that are distinctive of the Gospel rest on public events within history and not merely on private experiences (cf. Acts 26:26). Thus, Paul's argument ultimately turns on genuine faith in the prophets (cf. Acts 26:27).

In contrast to Festus, Agrippa did not accuse Paul of madness. Rather, he saw the force of Paul's argument and sought to sidestep it, exclaiming, "In a short time you think to make me a Christian!" (Acts 26:28). He realized that if he acknowledged the authority of the prophets, he would have accepted the foundation and hence the force of Paul's argument. In response, Paul openly confessed his desire that all who heard him should obtain the good of belief in Jesus (Acts 26:29). After Festus and Agrippa withdrew to discuss the case, they agreed that Paul had done "nothing to deserve death or imprisonment" (Acts 26:30–31).

*   *   *

## Questions for Discussion

**1.** Read Acts 26:8; Gal. 3:7–9; Heb. 11:17–19. In what ways is acceptance of the Resurrection of Christ the fundamental challenge of Abrahamic faith?

_____

_____

_____

_____

_____

_____

**2.** Read Acts 26:10–11, 14. Does Christ's admonition not "to kick against the goads" suggest that Paul felt the attraction of the Gospel even as he was persecuting the Church? If so, what factors might have led him to persecute the disciples so fiercely?

_____

_____

_____

_____

_____

_____

**3.** Read Acts 26:20–21; 2 Mac. 7:1–42. Why might Paul's opponents have been particularly disturbed by his evangelization among the Gentiles?

_____

_____

_____

_____

_____

_____

# 9

## AMONG THE ROMANS
### —ACTS 27–28—

Having granted Paul's appeal to the imperial court, Festus placed him in the custody of a centurion along with other prisoners with orders that they be transported to Rome (Acts 27:1). Thus commenced a remarkable and nearly disastrous voyage by sea that powerfully exemplifies God's providence to the eyes of faith. Although Paul and his companions came very close to death, God so guided the course of events that all of them were safely delivered. No miraculous interventions occurred during the sea voyage, yet through prayer and fortitude Paul eventually came to safety on land.

In accordance with ordinary Roman practice, the prisoners were transported on a commercial ship. Luke accompanied Paul, traveling with him again for the first time since they had arrived in Jerusalem (Acts 21:18). Aristarchus, a companion of Paul during his third journey (see Acts 19:29; 20:2–4), accompanied them as well (Acts 27:2). They first sailed north from Caesarea to Sidon, where the centurion allowed Paul to go ashore and visit the local church (Acts 27:3). Departing from Sidon to continue northward, they soon began to encounter unfavorable winds (Acts 27:4), and, turning west along the coast of Asia Minor, eventually came to the port of Myra (Acts 27:5). There, they disembarked from their original vessel and obtained passage on one of the many cargo ships that regularly sailed along the Mediterranean coast from Alexandria in Egypt to Rome to supply the capital with grain (cf. Acts 27:6).

## The Rage of the Sea

From Myra, they continued westward "with difficulty" until they reached Cnidus, at the southwestern corner of Asia Minor (Acts 27:7). From this point, a cargo ship would normally head directly across the Aegean Sea toward Greece, but the winds would not now permit this. Instead, they headed south to seek an easier passage along the southern coast of Crete. Again proceeding "with difficulty," they finally came to a Cretan harbor called the Fair Havens (Acts 27:8). At this point, "much time had been lost," as it had been almost forty days since the party left Caesarea, and the weather would only grow more dangerous for sailing, "because the fast had already gone by" (Acts 27:9). The "fast" was that required by the Mosaic Law for the Day of Atonement (see Lev. 16:29–31), which fell on the tenth of Tishri in the Hebrew calendar, in late September or early October. Sailing on the Mediterranean became extremely dangerous from around this time of year through January.

Due to previous hard experience, Paul knew well the unfriendliness of the sea (2 Cor. 11:25), and he advised the party not to press on (Acts 27:10). However, the Fair Havens was not a good harbor "to winter in," and so the ship's pilot and owner decided, with the centurion's concurrence, to try to reach a more suitable harbor on the western side of the island (Acts 27:11–12). They attempted to sail west along the southern coast, but were soon caught in a "tempestuous wind" and driven away from the island into open waters (Acts 27:13–15).

Paul's voyage now turned from bad to worse. The crew struggled throughout the day just to maintain control of the ship (cf. Acts 27:16–17). On the next day, they were so "violently storm-tossed" that they were forced to take desperate measures to lighten the ship, throwing overboard first the cargo and then the tackle (Acts 27:18–19). Nor did the storm soon abate but raged so fiercely that "for many a day" they saw "neither sun nor stars," until finally "all hope of our being saved was at last abandoned" (Acts 27:20).

### The Providence of God

At this point, concerned about their hunger and faltering morale, Paul stood to address the crew (cf. Acts 27:21). Speaking to the dispirited group of Gentile sailors and soldiers, Paul calmly declared that "the God to whom I belong and whom I worship" had sent an angel to inform him that none of them would die on this voyage, although there would be no easy landing and the ship would indeed be destroyed (Acts 27:22–24). Therefore, they should prepare themselves for the difficult finale of their journey (Acts 27:25–26).

During the "fourteenth night" of drifting, the sailors suspected and then verified that they were approaching land (Acts 27:27–28). However, this was no cause for joy, as they knew that in the dark the ship was in imminent danger of running on the rocks in shallow water. Under the pressure of the moment, the sailors responded with disgraceful self-interest and attempted surreptitiously to abandon the ship on the lifeboat, which they lowered while pretending to lower anchors. Paul quickly saw through the sailors' deception and informed the centurion of the ploy, which the soldiers then prevent-

ed by cutting the lifeboat loose (Acts 27:29–32).
Again, Paul assured the crew that their lives were safe
and urged them to eat in preparation for their landing
(Acts 27:33–34). To encourage them, he himself prepared to eat, giving thanks and breaking bread, as was
customary for Jews before meals (cf. Acts 27:35). The
crew did indeed eat before dumping the remaining
grain overboard (Acts 27:36–38).

The next morning, they could see a distant beach
and so attempted to land. However, as the crew had
feared, the ship struck a reef, grounded, and began to
break up (Acts 27:39–41). The only hope of survival
now was to swim for the beach, a possibility to which
the soldiers reacted with fear, not for their own imme-
diate safety, but for the ensuing loss of control of the
prisoners. Under Roman law, they would be held
liable for the escape of any prisoner and harshly pun-
ished. Rather than risk such an outcome, they
planned to kill the prisoners at once (Acts 27:42). The
centurion, however, did not wish to see Paul dead,
and blocked the soldiers' plan, instead ordering an
orderly evacuation of the ship, with those who could
swim going first, followed by those who needed the
assistance of floating debris from the ship. In the end,
just as Paul had foretold, all who had been on the ship
"escaped to land" (Acts 27:43–44).

## The Charity of Apostolate

The castaways discovered that they had come
ashore on the island of Malta (Acts 28:1). Luke refers
to the Maltese as *barbaroi*, or non-speakers of Greek,
because they were of Phoenician descent and
speech. The Maltese welcomed the party with kind-

ness and began building a fire for them (Acts 28:2). While helping to gather wood for the fire, Paul was bitten by a viper that "fastened on his hand" (Acts 28:3). Although he "shook off the creature into the fire" without difficulty, the Maltese were quite sure that Paul would "swell up or suddenly fall down dead" (Acts 28:5-6). When it finally became clear that Paul had suffered no harm, they judged his survival of the serpent's bite to be miraculous. Indeed, Paul's stay in Malta would be marked from beginning to end by the works of power that Jesus had conferred on the apostles (see Mk. 16:17-18; Lk. 10:18-19). He remained among the Maltese throughout the winter, laying hands on and healing first the father of "the chief man of the island" and then "the rest of the people on the island who had diseases" (Acts 28:7-9). As elsewhere in the apostles' ministry, these healings were a visible sign of the presence of the kingdom of God.

In the early months of AD 61, after three months on land, the party was given new provisions by their Maltese hosts and set sail on another ship from Alexandria. With his eye for colorful detail, Luke notes that the ship was dedicated to "the Twin Brothers," Castor and Pollux, the sons of Zeus, whose cult was popular in Alexandria and were thought to afford protection at sea (Acts 28:10-11). They sailed uneventfully to Syracuse, the leading city of Sicily, which, unlike Malta, was Greek-speaking (cf. Acts 28:12). After a few days, they sailed first to Rhegium, and then to Puteoli, the major port in southern Italy (Acts 28:13). At Puteoli, they stayed for a week with local disciples, who sent word ahead to the Roman church that Paul was on his way (Acts 28:14). Finally, the party set out for Rome itself.

When informed of the party's approach by the disciples from Puteoli, groups of disciples from Rome came down to meet the party as it traveled north on the Via Appia, the first group meeting the party at the Forum of Appius, forty miles south of Rome, and a second at the Three Taverns, thirty miles to the south (cf. Acts 28:15). The ready assistance given to Paul by the disciples at Puteoli and Rome illustrates the fraternal charity with which the apostolate was carried out.

### The Jews of Rome

Paul was well aware that the church had long been established in Rome (Rom. 1:8) and "for many years" had desired to visit it (Rom. 15:23–24). Arriving in the city, he was finally able to achieve his ambition. Although under house arrest and guarded by a soldier, he was allowed to live in privately rented lodgings (Acts 28:16). The relatively comfortable circumstances of his imprisonment reflected his status as a Roman citizen.

In Rome, unlike Jerusalem, Paul's ability to preach was unhindered. His first action was therefore to invite the "local leaders of the Jews" to his lodgings and request an opportunity to speak to their community. In accordance with his usual missionary custom, he wished first to proclaim the Gospel to the Jews of the locality before turning to the Gentiles. He stressed to the Jewish leaders his faithfulness to "the people" and to "the customs of our fathers." Yet, in spite of his faithfulness, he had been delivered by the Jerusalem leadership "into the hands of the Romans"

(Acts 28:17). Although he had no quarrel with his nation and the Romans had found him guilty of nothing, he was nevertheless forced by the persistent charges of the Jerusalem leadership to appeal to the imperial court (cf. Acts 28:18–19). The true reason that he was "bound with this chain" was his adherence to the "hope of Israel" in God's promise of covenantal restoration (Acts 28:20), the fulfillment of which has begun with the Resurrection of the Messiah (cf. Acts 26:6–8). For the sake of this hope, Paul wished to address the Jewish community.

## The Pattern of Isaiah

The Jewish leaders replied that they would gladly hear Paul expound his views, for they had neither received negative instructions nor heard anything unfavorable from Judea about him personally, although they were aware that the "sect" of Christians was "spoken against" by Jews "everywhere" (Acts 28:21–22). They therefore agreed upon a date, on which "great numbers" of the local Jews came to hear Paul speak. Paul followed his usual pattern for preaching in a synagogue, although he was confined to his own lodgings. Using arguments drawn from the Old Testament, he proclaimed the restoration of the kingdom of God through the person and work of Jesus (cf. Acts 28:23). As was often the case in response to the Gospel, some of the community "were convinced" and "others disbelieved" (Acts 28:24). Jesus had taught that the Gospel calls for a committed response from each person, so that those who accept it will be divided from those who reject it: "Do you think that I have come to give peace on earth? No, I tell you, but rather division; for henceforth in one house there will be five divided, three against two and two against three" (Lk. 12:51–52).

Paul's final statement applied the words of Isaiah's prophetic commission to those who rejected the Gospel (Acts 28:25–27; cf. Is. 6:9–10). Jesus had also used this passage from Isaiah to describe resistance to the Gospel (see Mt. 13:14–15; Mk. 4:11–12). In this passage, Isaiah is sent to recall the people of Judah to covenantal faithfulness but is warned by God from the beginning that many will not repent and Judah will be judged. The result of their rejection of the Word of God will be the conquest of Judah, the destruction of Jerusalem, and exile (cf. Is. 6:11–12). However, there will also be a remnant of the people, a "holy seed," who are faithful to God (Is. 6:13). The situation encountered by Isaiah will now be recapitulated in the ministry of the apostles. Just as Isaiah had to preach to the people of Judah in the face of the impending destruction of Jerusalem for the sake of the faithful remnant, Paul must now do the same. His mission of evangelism would continue unceasingly up to the very threshold of the Jewish War (AD 66), which would culminate in the destruction of the city and temple (AD 70).[1] Paul closed his final statement by declaring that God has proven utterly faithful to His Word by sending forth His message of salvation to all, first to Israel and then to the nations, who "will listen" (Acts 28:28).

---

[1] Josephus, *The Wars of the Jews* II:14–17; VI:4–9.

## Proclaiming the King

Although under house arrest for two years, Paul was able to pursue his apostolate "openly and unhindered" and did so energetically, proclaiming Jesus to be Lord of all in the very capital of the Roman empire (Acts 28:30–31). The Book of Acts thus concludes with a depiction of the testimony to Jesus, which began with the apostles "in Jerusalem and in all Judea and Samaria;" now moving "to the end of the earth" (Acts 1:8). Although eventually acquitted and released in AD 63, Paul was later arrested and put to death during the Neronian persecution of AD 66. In the midst of Nero's murderous persecution and the many to follow, the disciples maintained their faith that, through their faithful witness unto death, the kingdom of God would prevail over its enemies. As Paul had written to the Corinthians, the Resurrection of the Messiah inaugurated a reign in which the kingdom will advance until death itself is undone:

> But each in his own order: Christ the first fruits, then at his coming those who belong to Christ. Then comes the end, when he delivers the kingdom to God the Father after destroying every rule and every authority and power. For he must reign until he has put all his enemies under his feet. The last enemy to be destroyed is death. (1 Cor. 15:23–26)

\* \* \*

## Questions for Discussion

**1.** Read Acts 28:23. Do we study Scripture sufficiently to present the Gospel convincingly to those who do not yet have the faith but would be willing to listen?

_____

_____

_____

_____

_____

_____

**2.** Read Acts 28:24. How should Christians respond to the knowledge that some will reject the Gospel? Do we allow such rejection to become an impediment to our apostolates?

_____

_____

_____

_____

_____

_____

**3.** Read Acts 28:30–31. Paul proclaimed the Gospel in Rome while under house arrest for "two whole years," living "at his own expense." Do we allow adverse circumstances to become an excuse for passivity or inactivity in the apostolate?

_____

_____

_____

_____

_____